From
Faith to Faith

From
Faith to Faith

WATCHMAN NEE

Translated from the Chinese

Christian Fellowship Publishers, Inc.
New York

ISBN 0-935008-62-4

Available from the Publishers at:

11515 Allecingie Parkway
Richmond, Virginia 23235

TRANSLATOR'S PREFACE

"For [in the gospel] is revealed a righteousness of God from faith unto faith: as it is written, But the righteous shall live by faith" (Rom. 1.17). Thus declares the apostle Paul. In his explanation of this passage, John Calvin wrote: "*From* faith, for righteousness is offered by the gospel and is received by faith. *To* faith, for as our faith makes progress, and it advances in knowledge, so the righteousness of God increases in us at the same time, and the possession of it is in a manner confirmed."

In this present volume, Watchman Nee deals with various subjects which demonstrate this essential principle of "from faith to faith." He commences with such topics as "the truth shall make you free," the principle of the second, and circumcision—so as to unveil how the gospel of Jesus Christ is based on faith and not on works. He continues with such matters as God's will and man's willingness, the blood and worship, the seed of God, and the power of pressure—so as to disclose how the same gospel is to be experienced increasingly through faith in the Lord Jesus. Lastly, he concludes by contrasting Lot as a defeated righteous man with Enoch who by faith was translated that he should not see death.

All in all, this presentation can give us a right perspective of the gospel of Jesus Christ as well as help us to walk in the path of faith. "Now to him that is able to establish you according to my gospel and the preaching of Jesus Christ, . . . [which] is made known unto all the nations unto obedience of faith: to the only wise God, through Jesus Christ, to whom be glory forever. Amen" (Rom. 16.25–27).

CONTENTS

1 | The Truth Shall Make You Free

Ye shall know the truth, and the truth shall make you free. (John 8.32)

Over 1900 years ago Pontius Pilate asked this question of Jesus: "What is truth?" (John 18.38) This is also the question of many other people. We dare not explain what truth is in the Scripture according to our own idea, yet we do desire to find out from God's written word what it really is.

The word "truth" in Greek means "the reality lying at the basis of an appearance; the manifested, veritable essence of a matter" (Cremer). It means absolute reality; it is "true" and "real." We may not know the reason of many true things, yet they are facts and realities which we may touch.

"The law was given through Moses; grace and truth came through Jesus Christ" (John 1.17). Grace is not an attitude of God; it is a work of God. Grace is the

work which Jesus of Nazareth the Son of God has accomplished for us. The Son of God was crucified for
us; He shed His blood to accomplish God's work of
redemption so that we would not need to do anything
but to trust Him and be saved. Without the work of
the cross, God has no way to give grace to men. He
gave law to men through Moses, but He gives grace
through the finished work of the cross. Hence, grace
is the work of God.

Moreover, in the same sentence from John 1, we read
of both grace and truth. For truth as well as grace comes
from the Lord Jesus. When God gave His only begotten Son to the world, He appointed Him to be truth
as much as grace. Both grace and truth come through
the work of the Son of God. Without His work, there
would be neither grace nor truth today. For the Lord
Jesus must create grace in order to grant grace. This
is what all Christians believe. In like manner, it is required of the Lord Jesus to create truth before He can
disperse truth. Thus it is written, "even as truth is in
Jesus" (Eph. 4.21). Hence God works out truth in the
Lord Jesus. Truth is in the Lord Jesus, and truth is His
work.

"I am the truth," declared the Lord Jesus (John
14.6). Truth in the Scriptures has no other meaning than
reality. What is reality? Reality is what I actually am
before God as a result of the accomplished work of
Christ. The Lord Jesus shed His blood to ransom all
who belong to Him. This is a fact. Through Christ I
am a redeemed soul before God. This is the truth. What
I am through the fact accomplished by the Lord
Jesus — that is the truth. Consequently, only after Jesus

has accomplished a work will I have the truth. Without His work, I will have no truth, no reality. I was originally a dead person, a sinner in God's sight. I had neither position nor possession before Him. But now, thank God, due to the work of the Lord Jesus, I have reality before God. I have obtained something real, and that reality is that I am a redeemed person.

Let us keep well in mind that the truth as given in the Bible does not refer to the doctrine preached from the pulpit but to the fact before God. Doctrine is something people try to explain on earth; truth is what I become before God owing to what the Lord Jesus has accomplished. Through the work of Christ, God has transformed me to be another person. And such is the truth; such is the reality. We must remember that the work of Jesus Christ has already been accomplished before God and that what becomes of me through that finished work is the truth. For the truth is none other than Christ himself. All realities are in Christ, all facts are in Christ.

The Truth Sets Us Free

Have we not obtained the truth? Here arises a problem: you discover that what you are before God and what you are on earth are totally different. The work of the cross is finished, but you are still undone. The kind of person Christ transforms is not the same person you are on earth. This is to say that your own condition does not agree with the truth before God. And this is where the difficulty lies.

Oftentimes we do not know what truth is. As we

approach God, we rely on our own feeling rather than
on the truth of God, on our own experience rather than
on His truth. Let us realize, however, that God's truth
opposes your feeling and your experience. The solution
to the matter is to recognize what is true. Which is true:
that which the Lord Jesus has accomplished before God
for me or that which I feel or experience?

How frequently we are bound because we fail to see
what is true, what is the reality. Yet as soon as we shall
see the truth, the truth shall make us free. Let me mention a few things which can serve to illustrate how the
truth sets us free.

We will begin with salvation. Suppose a certain person accepts Christ after he has heard how the Lord Jesus
died on the cross and shed His blood for the forgiveness
of his sins. If he is asked whether he now belongs to
the Lord, he will unhesitatingly answer that he does indeed belong to Him. He feels so happy within that he
almost explodes. Three or five months then pass. His
health declines and his family has problems. He finds
that his joy has left him. He does not look like a saved
person, a child of God. If he were asked during that
time whether he is a Christian, a saved soul, he would
probably reply: "I am puzzled, for my former joy is lost.
I do not even know where the Lord Jesus has gone. I
do not know what to say." How would you deal with
him? If you know the truth of God, you would say to
him, "According to your feeling you may seem *un*saved,
but according to fact and reality you *are* saved."

It actually depends upon from which perspective
you are looking. From one perspective you might indeed think the brother is not saved; but viewed from

the perspective of the work of Christ, you would tell him: "Brother, there is no change. You are saved. When you feel warm you are saved; and when you feel cold, you are still saved. Your feeling may change, but what God has given you through the work of Christ never changes. Hence, always try to look from that vantage point." "Ye shall know the truth," declares the Lord, "and the truth shall make you free." As one's eyes are opened to perceive that which is obtained before God through the work of the Lord Jesus, he sees the truth, the reality. And that will set him free. May we always remember that we do not obtain freedom by our feeling, since the one and only thing which makes us free is the reality before God.

There once was a brother who had truly repented, believed in the Lord, and had been regenerated. After a while his feeling within him suffered a change. He felt inwardly terrible, and therefore he concluded he would perish. Another brother asked him, "How do you know you will perish?" "I am different from what I was before," answered that brother. "I feel icy cold inside, and my prayer and Bible reading are weak." "But that is viewing the matter from the condition of your side," observed the second brother. "Let us instead look at a few things from God's side: Has the work of the Lord been discounted? Has the work of Christ changed?" "No, it has not," replied the first brother. "Has the New Covenant been abrogated?" "No." "Good, then," continued the second brother, "it is now ascertained that there has been no change on God's side. And thus, according to the truth—according to reality—you have not been changed from being saved to being unsaved.

You may *feel* you have changed; but that is only your feeling. Irrespective of how you feel, God has declared that you are saved. Will that be subject to change? Remember that salvation is a matter of truth, not one of feeling." After the first brother heard this, tears ran down his face as he said, "It really does not matter how I feel or what I say; God says that I am saved, so I am saved." Now this is how the truth can set a person free. Spiritual reality delivers people from their own feeling and sets them free.

Let us take a step further to see how the truth makes us free. God's word not only shows us how our sins are forgiven and we are regenerated through Christ's bearing our sins on the cross; it also shows us that in the death of Christ, God has put us in Him so that our old man was crucified with Him. His death is not the death of a single person, it is instead a corporate death. When Jesus died on the cross, we died in Him. On the ground of what Christ has accomplished, we are already dead. This is the truth, this is reality.

Before we saw this truth, we were bound. As we looked at ourselves, we saw our ill temper. As we touched ourselves, we touched weakness. We felt there was nothing good in us from head to toe. So that the question is, which is real: our feeling and experience, or the work of Christ? How many tears are shed because we feel nothing more real than this bondage of self. Yet the word of God shows us that only one thing is real, and that is, what His Son has done. Our old man was crucified with Christ. This is the truth. Failing to see this truth makes us a slave to our ill temper or whatever. We are bound by our own experience and feeling.

What can make a person free? Only the truth can make one free, only the reality can set one free. If anyone relies on his own feeling and experience he will constantly be defeated. But if he sees the fact of his co-death with Christ, that person will be set free.

Let us look at still another matter, that of the victory of the Lord Jesus. Once upon a time there was a brother who for several months was attacked by Satan both physically and mentally. He tried his very best to resist the enemy with prayer. But in spite of his earnest prayers, the attack continued. One evening he told the Lord: "I cannot resist any more because my strength is exhausted. I cannot pray any longer because I have used up all my praying strength. Lord, show me where the root of this situation lies." Immediately God opened his eyes and gave him a word. He had seen the word before, although seeing it as through dense woods. Now he saw it clearly. And the word was simply this: "Is Satan worth my resisting?" He had never thought that resisting Satan could be a resisting wrongly. But that evening he saw the reality. The reality is, that Christ has already overcome; and since I am united with Him, I too have overcome. It does not say the Lord Jesus *will* overcome, and that I am therefore to try to hasten Him somewhat. It plainly says that He *has* overcome. Neither does it say Satan shall be defeated, so that I now am to ask the Lord to defeat him. Praise and thank the Lord, Satan is already defeated. It is *done*, not that it *shall* be done. Now as this brother began to see the truth, the attack stopped on that very evening. Everything became normal. This is how reality sets people free.

Truth and Light

In order to see the truth of God, we need His enlightenment. "Send out thy light and thy truth " (Ps. 43.3). What does the light of God shine upon? God uses light to shine upon His truth. This is of great importance, since we know God's truth through enlightenment. Truth is not obtained through preaching; it comes from the enlightenment of God.

Suppose you ask brothers and sisters if they have died in Christ. Perhaps many will answer that they have died yet they do not understand why this does not work in their lives. This is because they have heard the teaching but have not seen the truth. Whoever sees the reality is the one who has received the enlightenment.

A brother once testified that after God had opened his eyes to see Romans 6, he was also given to see Ephesians 6. He saw his death as a fact, but he also saw the victory of Christ as a fact. He was thus made partaker of the victory of Christ. What he had long expected was now something he at last realized he had already obtained. Formerly he had hoped the Lord would give him victory; now he praised the Lord, declaring that the Lord had already overcome. He bore witness to the vast difference between this life and his old life. Formerly, it had been admirations and expectations; today it was reality. Not something to grasp at, but something already in hand. Whenever light comes, a person will leap and cry aloud that it is done!

Every Christian has seen light. He saw the light at least once while he was being saved. When one is saved, he sees that he is not expecting salvation or eternal life as something of the *future*; rather, he praises and thanks God for what Christ has *already done*. In thus seeing the light shining upon reality, one becomes a Christian. All Christians have seen the light enlightening this reality. All spiritual experience comes through light shining upon the truths.

Consequently, when truth is preached, it becomes doctrine if there is no enlightenment. But when it is preached with the light of God shining upon it, this truth becomes a revelation. Having revelation is possessing truth. All who have doctrines have their minds full of ideas; but all who have revelation have life and reality.

The Spirit of Truth and the Word of Truth

When we receive enlightenment from God, we are brought into spiritual reality. We ought to know that on the one hand there is the Spirit of truth, who is the Comforter; and on the other hand, there is the word of truth, the Bible, which tells us the true facts of salvation God has accomplished in Christ. As we believe in these words of truth, the Holy Spirit brings us into these truths — into reality. The Lord Jesus is that reality. And God through the Holy Spirit brings us into reality so that what we have is no longer simply doctrine or teaching. We shall no longer live in our own feeling or

experience; rather, we shall live in the facts which Christ
has accomplished for us.

Therefore, the important question is: is there revelation? For when you receive revelation, you will not think
of your own experience nor pay attention to your own
feeling; instead, you will believe that what is from God
is absolutely certain and secure. How many Christians
feel their old man is well and alive! And they dare not
assert that they have already died with Christ. But
revelation will change them. Revelation will enable them
to see that their old man is dead indeed. Only those
who have the revelation of the Holy Spirit may enter
into that reality. The Holy Spirit reveals to the believer
the reality so that he dares to proclaim the truth of it.

True experience follows after seeing what God has
done. May He open our eyes to see what truth is. If
we really see the truth, the truth shall make us free. Our
freedom comes from the truth. Therefore, let us seek
for truth, which means to seek for reality. May the
revelation of God brings us into that reality.

2 | The Principle of the Second

So also it is written, The first man Adam became a living soul. The last Adam became a life-giving spirit. Howbeit that is not first which is spiritual, but that which is natural; then that which is spiritual. The first man is of the earth, earthy: the second man is of heaven. (1 Cor. 15.45-47)

Abraham said unto God, O that Ishmael might live before thee! And God said, Nay, but Sarah thy wife shall bear thee a son; and thou shalt call his name Isaac: and I will establish my covenant with him for an everlasting covenant for his seed after him. (Gen. 17.18,19)

Jehovah said unto her, Two nations are in thy womb, and two peoples shall be separated from thy bowels: and the one people shall be stronger than the other people; and the elder shall serve the younger. (Gen. 25.23)

It was said unto her, The elder shall serve the younger. Even as it is written, Jacob I loved, but Esau I hated. (Rom. 9.12,13)

Joseph said unto his father, Not so, my father; for

this is the first-born; put thy right hand upon his head. And his father refused, and said, I know it, my son, I know it; he also shall become a people, and he also shall be great: howbeit his younger brother shall be greater than he, and his seed shall become a multitude of nations. (Gen. 48.18,19)

They said unto him, Behold, thou art old, and thy sons walk not in thy ways: now make us a king to judge us like all the nations. (1 Sam. 8.5)

Jehovah said unto Samuel, How long wilt thou mourn for Saul, seeing I have rejected him from being king over Israel? fill thy horn with oil, and go: I will send thee to Jesse the Bethlehemite; for I have provided me a king among his sons. (1 Sam. 16.1)

Howbeit, because by this deed thou hast given great occasion to the enemies of Jehovah to blaspheme, the child also that is born unto thee shall surely die. . . . And David comforted Bathsheba his wife, and went in unto her, and lay with her: and she bare a son, and he called his name Solomon. And Jehovah loved him; and he sent by the hand of Nathan the prophet; and he called his name Jedidiah, for Jehovah's sake. (2 Sam. 12.14, 24, 25)

These passages in the Bible present to us a revealed principle of God. We may call this "the principle of the second," or "the law of the second."

God Always Chooses the Second

From these passages we may learn that what God chooses is always the second, not the first. 1 Corinthians 15 tells us that the first is of the earth, but the second is of heaven. The first is natural, while the second is spiritual. I myself often wonder why it is that in the Scriptures God seems always to choose the second person. Ishmael is the elder son, yet God chooses Isaac the younger son. Esau is the older brother, but God chooses Jacob the younger brother. Later on, we learn that though Ephraim is the second son while Manasseh is the firstborn, God nevertheless chooses Ephraim. Bathsheba gave birth to two children, but God smote the first child while He loved the second child Solomon. He loved Solomon so much that He sent the prophet Nathan to give another name to him, the name Jedidiah—which means "beloved of the Lord" (and note that according to the flesh, our Lord came from this very root). Furthermore, the first king, Saul, is rejected by God; but David, who was the second king, is chosen by God, for He declares that David is a man after His own heart (Acts 13.22).

Why God Rejects the First and Accepts the Second

Why is it that God rejects the elder and accepts the younger? Why does He hate the first one and love the second one? The answer to this is what we now wish to search out.

Let us note that God deals this way with sinners as well as with Israel and believers. Why in Exodus did God command the children of Israel to put blood on the two side posts and on the lintel of their doors for the sake of the firstborn? Why were the firstborn exposed to danger, but the secondborn were not? Why

in the Bible must all the firstborn of the herds and the
flocks be redeemed, otherwise they would have their
necks broken (for when the neck is broken, the central
nervous system is broken, and that spells death)? Why
must the firstborn, not the secondborn, of the herds
and the flocks be ransomed? Yet not just the firstborn
of the herds and the flocks must be redeemed, even the
firstborn of the children of Israel must be redeemed
(the second child need not be redeemed). For if the
firstborn is not redeemed, he will be cut off and will
not be reckoned among God's people. Why is God
especially displeased with the firstborn? or why does
He particularly love the second son and show special
favor to him? Why does He take the entire tribe of Levi
instead of the firstborn among all the children of Israel,
and why does He require the odd number to be redeemed with shekels (see Num. 3.44-51)?

We know the record of the Bible is never casually
set down. The way it is recorded indicates a most vital
principle. Though such a principle may not be universally recognized, we are nonetheless sure that God never
does anything arbitrarily. Once, twice, and many times
over He does something in a particular manner in order
to show us where His way lies. For His "acts" are governed by His "ways." We will make great progress in
knowing God and spiritual things if we learn this principle and the way of God.

What really *is* implied in God rejecting the first and
accepting the second? Let us read again 1 Corinthians
15.46: "Howbeit that is not first which is spiritual, but
that which is natural; then that which is spiritual." We
realize that this chapter deals with the resurrection of

the body. Our purpose in reading this passage, however, lies not in investigating the resurrection of the body but in understanding some spiritual principle. According to this passage, the natural body comes first, and then comes the spiritual body. Hence we may say that the spiritual principle here is that the spiritual always comes afterwards whereas the natural always comes first. This, then, explains why God chooses the second and rejects the first.

What is the first one? "Jesus answered and said unto him, Verily, verily, I say unto thee, Except one be born anew, he cannot see the kingdom of God. . . . That which is born of the flesh is flesh; and that which is born of the Spirit is spirit" (John 3.3,6). Our Lord is talking about being born again. He implies that being born once is not good enough, one must be born again. He who is born only once cannot see the kingdom of God and is reckoned as useless. Only he who is born anew has eternal life and may see the kingdom of God. He then explains what is meant by the first birth. It is that which is born of the flesh. But what is meant by the second birth? It is that which is born of the Spirit. Consequently, whatever is born of the flesh — whatever is endowed naturally — belongs to the first; but that whatever does not come by means of the flesh but comes by being born of the Holy Spirit belongs to the second.

Let us see how much is included in the phrase "that which is born of the flesh." All that I inherit from the parents who beget me — such things as affection, talent, cleverness, gentleness, humbleness, love, peace, determination, and patience — these all, and more, come with my natural birth. Whatever I have before the new birth, and no matter how lovely it is viewed in human eyes, is included by the words of the Lord Jesus as being in this realm: that " that which is born of the flesh *is* flesh." For this reason, we need to ask ourselves whether all that we have after new birth is born of God. Or does that which I have still include that which is born of the flesh? Let us not reason that only the sins and uncleannesses of the flesh need to be eliminated, whereas natural gentleness, patience, loving-kindness, cleverness, and talent can all be retained and carried over without ever being born anew of God. Who among us truly recognizes that all which we inherit from the first—that is to say, from that which is of the flesh—must be denied and laid down? Let us humbly acknowledge that only what comes from believing in the Lord Jesus, from trusting in God, and from appropriating through the Holy Spirit is acceptable and pleasing to God.

Therefore, the first matter of importance is for a person to be born again. Blessed is he who has two lives and two natures. Someone may confess the Lord Jesus with his mouth and even go to church service, but all that he naturally has is from his parents, and he is consequently still a perishing sinner. What one naturally possesses and learns is hopeless and useless before God. But if a person believes in the Lord, he will possess what comes of the second—even eternal life.

Christians today must learn how to distinguish between the first and the second, between what is given to us by our parents and what is given to us by God through the Holy Spirit. Unfortunately, many believers do not have this clear understanding. They are unable to differentiate the first from the second, unable to discern what comes from the first and what comes from the second. They assume that as long as they are zealous and patient, as long as their speech is proper and their prayer is good, that their lives and works will be acceptable.

Permit me to say that I know whereof I speak. God never looks at good works *per se*; He only looks at the *source* of those good works. What is the source of *your* good works? It is not that God does not require gentleness, but that He asks where that gentleness comes from. Does it come from your self or from the Holy Spirit? From where does your zeal actually originate? From your self or from the Holy Spirit? What is the underlying principle in asking such questions? It revolves, quite plainly, around this issue of the first or the second: God always rejects the first but approves the second.

To illustrate. I have a quick temper. When I see patience in other people, I admire it and speak well of it. But God will probe more deeply with the question: from where does that patience originate? As soon as we see any good in "the first" we immediately pronounce it as good. Yet God will not pronounce it good until He sees that it has come from Him. And then we can be sure that what *He* says is good is good indeed. When we observe a preacher who speaks boldly and works actively, we may conclude that he is spiritual. But God wants to know if these qualities come from "the first" or from "the second." One dear brother has related how undiscerning certain Christians were by their pronounc-

ing a preacher to be powerful if he beat the lectern with
his fists. We should ask, however, where the power
manifested has come from. We cannot rely on talent,
power or nature which comes from the first. Only that
which emerges after the new birth comes from the second, and is thus acceptable to God.

The Principle of the Second
Applies to All Believers

This principle applies to every believer and not
merely to preachers. Any natural goodness — for example, patience — is like a rubber band which can only be
stretched to a certain length; it will soon reach its break-
ing point and will never be able to carry on with God.
Quite differently, though, if the natural goodness (in
this case patience) comes from God, for it may be
stretched and stretched as long as is required. Let it be
clearly understood that natural resources cannot supply
spiritual needs. What is of the first, Adam, can never
help what is of the second, Christ. Oh, how many think
that as long as they love people, they are all right. But
is it all right? Does this love come from God?

One brother has said that only what comes from
heaven may return to heaven. We consider heaven our
home because we and all we have come from heaven.
So that a returning to heaven is said to be a returning
home. Yet if what we have is not heavenly but earthly,
then heaven will be our hotel instead of our home. It
is certain that God will not receive back to himself what
has not come out from Him.

Let us ask ourselves this: are there changes in our

lives since we have believed? In being a Christian, does it only mean our getting rid of sins, failures, weaknesses and uncleannesses of the past? It is well that these are eliminated; God, however, makes it plain in His word that this is not enough. He not only calls the obviously bad things no good but also labels the so-called good things of the flesh as no good too. He declares that He has no need of the first — *in its entirety.* He rejects the cleverness of the flesh as much as the gross sins of the flesh. He denounces the good of the flesh as well as the uncleanness of the flesh. He is displeased with everything that comes out of the natural life. Nothing of the old can be mixed with the new.

In the Gospels we read of our Lord Jesus saying: "He that loveth father or mother more than me is not worthy of me; and he that loveth son or daughter more than me is not worthy of me" (Matt. 10.37). We read that He further says: "If any man cometh unto me, and hateth not his own father, and mother, and wife, and children, and brethren, and sisters, yea, and his own life also, he cannot be my disciple" (Luke 14.26). Yet our Lord through one of Paul's epistles not only exhorts the children to obey their parents but also exhorts the parents not to provoke their children to wrath (see Eph. 6.1-4). The Lord also shows us the proper relationship between husband and wife: how husbands should love their own wives, and wives their own husbands (see Eph. 5.22,25). The Gospels dwell on hate, whereas the Epistles dwell on love. Unless you are able to distinguish between "the first" and "the second" — between that which is of the flesh and that which is of the Spirit — you will not understand why; for when

you hear the Lord say "he that loveth his father or
mother more than me is not worthy of me," you might
infer that you can treat your family carelessly and
callously; or when you hear Paul say that the family
members must love one another, you might conclude
that you must love your family members above everything else. You do not realize, however, that what the
Lord warns against is natural love, and what Paul exhorts you to cultivate is spiritual love. If your love is
natural, your love for your family will draw you away
from the Lord until your communion with Him and
love for Him will be greatly reduced if not eliminated
altogether. But if you are willing to commit your father
and mother and wife and children to God, being willing even to hate them if He wills, than you shall immediately perceive the second commandment of God—
which is, to love your father and mother and wife and
children. For you will have then been freed from "the
first" and can now enter into the experience of "the second." What error people commit when they accept only
the Gospel half or the Epistle half of the New
Testament.

Must Continually Be Delivered from the First

Our lives and labors must continually be delivered
from the first. Perhaps I can illustrate it this way. It
is relatively easy to understand the two terms, fleshly
and spiritual, in the abstract; but it is fairly difficult
to distinguish them in terms of practical living. How
can we know which good comes from the first and
which good comes from the second? Is there any mark

by which we can recognize them? Let me lay down a cardinal rule here: that whatever is spiritual has been through death (I believe all who are experienced in this matter will say amen). In other words, that which is spiritual is that which has been resurrected. Whatever originates with natural birth without experiencing the intervention of God's supernatural power belongs to the first: all the cleverness, lovingkindness, goodness, or talent which one possesses from birth until the time of believing the Lord is reckoned by God to be fleshly. Nothing during this period pleases God. But after a person believes in the Lord Jesus, then whatever is added to that one by God through the Holy Spirit belongs to the second; he has denied with singlemindedness all his natural goodness and talent—having considered them to be undependable—and now relies instead on the Holy Spirit for guidance, strength and victory so as to live out Christ. Whatever is of the second, whatever is of God, requires the believer to lay down his own wisdom, strength and natural talent. That which we obtain after such denial is the resurrected, the spiritual, and the second.

How very little we possess of the God-given second! How rarely we live by the life of the second! What the usual practice with us is that we eliminate the bad of the first but use the good of the first. God makes it clear, however, that our natural cleverness, talent, gentleness and lovingkindness must also pass through death even as our corruption, uncleanness and sin need to be eliminated. Perhaps, though, we may speculate as follows: Will we not be fools if we do not use our natural cleverness? Will we not be hard-hearted if we do not use our natural gentleness? Yet the Bible's answer is that God wants all of these to pass through death. Suppose, for example, that I am most clever. With my cleverness I can discover many new ideas from the Bible. But if I wish to live according to the principle of the second, I will not depend upon my cleverness; I will instead rely on God completely. Whether I am reading the Scriptures or praying, I will trust in God, just as God's word says: "apart from me ye can do nothing" (John 15.5). And thus shall you discover that you have passed through death. You have laid down your very self in this area. And in so doing you will come to see how God begins to use your renewed cleverness. Whatever has passed through death, that is to say, has gone through the cross, is desired by God and will be used by Him.

The Life of the Second — Painful to the Flesh

Be aware, of course, that the flesh will most assuredly cry out: "What a painful life this is! I will not have any liberty to act as quickly as I wish; I must instead wait on God! I will have to acknowledge my corruption and uselessness and spend time in prayer!" Yet we need to be reminded that this kind of life is fruit bearing: "Except a grain of wheat fall into the earth and die, it abideth by itself alone; *but if it die, it beareth much fruit*" (John 12.24). Despite the word of their Lord, however, many believers refuse to assume this attitude. With the result that all their lives they live in the first. They have never known or little known the life in the second. Their natural life refuses to pass through death. They may appear quite good outwardly, but they cannot bear real spiritual fruit.

Let me use the Lord Jesus himself as an illustration. Our Lord when on earth never knew what sin was. Even had He spoken out from himself, all which He would have done on that basis would still have been good, simply because He was sinless, pure, and without blemish: His life and nature are perfect. Nevertheless, as He walked on earth the Lord Jesus repeatedly declared: "The Son can do nothing of himself, but what he seeth the Father doing: for what things soever he doeth, these the Son also doeth in like manner" (John 5.19). Why did He not do anything out from himself? Simply because He saw that that would have been done in the natural realm and not something done by the Father. If someone so naturally perfect and pure and beautiful as the Lord Jesus could not do anything from himself, how much more needful is it that *we* not try to do anything from ourselves. If He who himself came from heaven would not rely upon His perfect flesh but relied instead upon the Holy Spirit, how much more ought *we* to depend upon the Holy Spirit.

Whatever the Lord Jesus did He did according to God's will, relying in the process on the power of the Holy Spirit. And thus He shows us the fact that even a being without sin is not something good enough before God. Our lives must overcome the natural goodness as well as overcome sin and uncleanness. How the life of God in us is oppressed by our natural life! Our lives and works are governed too much by our own thoughts. We trust too much in our own wisdom and strength in the service of God. God's call today is for us to come before Him with such singleness of mind that we reckon all which is of the natural to be futile. In response let us humble and empty ourselves before Him in order that we may completely trust and obey Him.

We acknowledge such a way is painful to the flesh. It is a life dependent and humble. Yet if we wish to live by the life of the second, we must live daily in humility as captives of God. Nonetheless, such a life pleases God greatly and such work has spiritual effectiveness.

In conclusion let me say that whatever may be done or can be done without the need of prayer or dependence on the power of the Holy Spirit will not please God but is condemned by Him because it must be of the flesh. May all that we are and have be that which comes from humbly trusting in God. May we daily put the natural life to death by the life of God until the day of the Lord's return. May God's new creation swallow up our old creation.

3 | Circumcision

In him ye are made full, who is the head of all prin-
cipality and power: in whom ye were also circumcised with
a circumcision not made with hands, in the putting off
of the body of the flesh, in the circumcision of Christ;
having been buried with him in baptism, wherein ye were
also raised with him through faith in the working of God,
who raised him from the dead. And you, being dead
through your trespasses and the uncircumcision of your
flesh, you, I say, did He make alive together with him,
having forgiven us all our trespasses.(Col. 2.10-13)

When Abram was ninety years old and nine, Jehovah
appeared to Abram, and said unto him, I am God
Almighty; walk before me, and be thou perfect.(Gen. 17.1)

God said unto Abraham, And as for thee, thou shalt
keep my covenant, thou, and thy seed after thee
throughout their generations. This is my covenant, which
ye shall keep, between me and you and thy seed after thee:
every male among you shall be circumcised. And ye shall

be circumcised in the flesh of your foreskin; and it shall be a token of a covenant betwixt me and you. And he that is eight days old shall be circumcised among you, every male throughout your generations, he that is born in the house, or bought with money of any foreigner that is not of thy seed. He that is born in thy house, and he that is bought with thy money, must needs be circumcised: and my covenant shall be in your flesh for an everlasting covenant. And the uncircumcised male who is not circumcised in the flesh of his foreskin, that soul shall be cut off from his people; he hath broken my covenant. (vv. 9-14)

He left off talking with him, and God went up from Abraham. And Abraham took Ishmael his son, and all that were born in his house, and all that were bought with his money, every male among the men of Abraham's home, and circumcised the flesh of their foreskin in the selfsame day, as God had said unto him.(vv. 22,23)

"In whom [Christ] ye [Christians] were also circumcised with a circumcision not made with hands, in the putting off of the body of the flesh, in the circumcision of Christ" (Col. 2.11). We know by this word that we Christians have been circumcised with a circumcision not made with hands. This means that one part of the inheritance which Christians have in Christ is the circumcision in Christ. Some may not understand what circumcision is. So let us return to Genesis 17 since circumcision is there mentioned for the first time in the Scriptures. By understanding what it says there, we will understand what is said here in Colossians chapter 2.

Some background may be necessary to our understanding. At this juncture Abraham was already 99 years old (Gen. 17.1). More than a decade earlier, before he was 86, he was promised by God to have a son and to be the father of a nation. Nevertheless, he considered himself too old and his wife beyond the possibility of conception. It was hopeless to him. So Sarah suggested that he take her maid Hagar as concubine. They conspired by fleshly means to help God fulfill his promise. Abraham at the age of 86 fathered a son by Hagar and named him Ishmael (16.16).

How did God react to this situation? For He had neither ordained it that way nor desired their fleshly help. Since they trusted in their flesh, God grew cold towards them. Concerning the 13 years between Abraham's 86th and 99th years, nothing was recorded in Scripture, which indicates that there was no communion with God. At the age of 86, Abraham still had procreative strength, but at 99 his strength was exhausted, beyond any hope. God waited until that time to make a covenant with him, a covenant which required that all males who belonged to Abraham must be circumcised. And a year after the establishment of that covenant, Sarah gave birth to Isaac. First there was the pronouncement of circumcision and then came the birth of Isaac. Without circumcision, there could be no Isaac.

Hereby may we understand why God ordered circumcision. What God would now perform was to be just the opposite to what Abraham had done. When Abraham was 86 he could still use his fleshly strength and try human ways. But at 99, he looked upon himself as hopeless. If anything was now to be done, the *Almighty God* would himself have to do it. On this very occasion the descriptive title of "God Almighty" was used for the first time and recorded in the Bible. For by that time Abraham understood that except for the power of the Almighty, man had absolutely no strength. And such is the meaning of circumcision.

One—The Punishment for Not Being Circumcised

"The uncircumcised male who is not circumcised in the flesh of his foreskin, that soul shall be cut off from his people; he hath broken my covenant" (Gen. 17.14). By this statement we are given to understand that all who remained uncircumcised were not reckoned to be God's people and would therefore have no dealings with God. They are not considered to be the seed of Abraham, and were accordingly not included in the Abrahamic Covenant.

Two—The Nature of Circumcision

"He that is eight days old shall be circumcised among you, every male throughout your generations" (17.12a). We know what constitutes circumcision: a piece of skin is cut away from the body and thrown out. But why does God make a human body and then demand that a piece of its skin be cut off? When a child is born, is he not God's beautiful creation? Indeed, he is. Then why, if God gives life to this child, does He require man to perform an additional work of cutting off a piece of skin? Why does God himself not effect circumcision upon the child before he is born? Why does He instead require man to cut away this skin? And why must a child be circumcised on the *eighth* day. Well, we know that the eighth day is representative of the day of the resurrection of our Lord. And hence, to be circumcised on the eighth day means to cut off the lusts and passions of our flesh through the resurrection power of Christ. The basic meaning of circumcision is thus the cutting off of the lusts and passions of the flesh.

Yet why does not God require a child to be circumcised on the day he is born rather than on the eighth day of his life? Here we may see the difference between creation and redemption, between the natural and the resurrected. According to our understanding of the gospel, God does not make anyone a Christian the moment he is born—that is to say, He does not give that one a spiritual life. Even a child born of the best parents must be born again, for upon that child there is only God's creative power and not His redemptive power as well. He is created by God, but he does not have God's life which is resurrection life. The most beautiful creature in the world is a new-born baby. He seems so innocent. Yet under God's old covenant, if he had not— naturally speaking—been circumcised on the eighth day, he would have been cut off from God's people. Spiritually speaking, under the new covenant of God, the same thing would be true if he were not circumcised in Christ.

Perhaps you are naturally good and gentle and undisturbed by sins. You may even consider yourself morally superior to other people. If, though, you have not been circumcised, you are not numbered among God's people. If a new-born baby needs to be circumcised, how much more do you and I need to be circumcised? If a child must be circumcised on the eighth day, how much more must you and I be circumcised after we have been on earth for several decades? Who can measure how defiled our hands and feet are? Ought we not to be circumcised on the eighth day? No one can meet God in his natural state. No matter how much of the gospel we have heard, we will not escape perishing if we are not circumcised; for man will indeed perish if left to his natural state.

Three — Who Must Be Circumcised

"Every male throughout your generations, he that is born in the house, or bought with money of any foreigner that is not of thy seed" (17.12b). In the old days two kinds of people needed to be circumcised: the one kind consisted of those who had been born in the house, and the other, of those who had been bought with money. Whether they were born or were purchased, they had to be circumcised. Praise God, we of today have been born of God as well as bought or redeemed by God. For notice the following two sets of verses from the New Testament which bear this out: (1) "Knowing that ye are redeemed, not with corruptible things, with silver or gold, from your vain manner of life handed down from your fathers; but with precious blood, as of a lamb without blemish and without spot, even the blood of Christ" (1 Peter 1.18,19); "ye were bought with a price" (1 Cor. 6.20). These verses speak of our being purchased and redeemed by God. And (2) "That which is born of the Spirit is spirit" (John 3.6); "whosoever is begotten of God" (1 John 3.9). These verses clearly bespeak the fact of our being born of God.

We thank the Lord that though God has not made a covenant with us non-Jews, we Gentiles nonetheless have the possibility of being circumcised: "When a stranger shall sojourn with thee, and will keep the passover to Jehovah, let all his males be circumcised, and then let him come near and keep it; and he shall be as one that is born in the land" (Ex. 12.48). This passage informs us that a Gentile stranger may also be circumcised. If there is any reader who has not yet believed in the Lord Jesus, let me say that you too can be circumcised today if you so will, and can be like the other children of God today who have been circumcised in Christ.

Four—The Meaning of Circumcision

Circumcision, as was stated earlier, means the cutting off of the passions and lusts of the flesh. No one can serve God with his flesh: "The flesh," declared Jesus, "profiteth nothing" (John 6.63); and according to Paul in Romans 8.7, "the mind of the flesh is enmity against God." We need to cut off the flesh if we ever want to serve God and have a part in His covenant.

What is meant by the flesh? That which one inherits at birth, that which he naturally possesses, that which an unbeliever owns. Such flesh, whether it is good or bad, must be circumcised, because the flesh will neither be subject to God nor can it be. Even the good done by the flesh is not able to please God. After we have believed in the Lord Jesus, we must receive the circumcision of the heart if we expect God's pleasure. The children of Abraham received circumcision in their body; we must receive circumcision in our heart.

Yet circumcision of the heart is not only a matter spoken of in the New Testament (this we might reasonably expect), it is also mentioned—perhaps surprisingly to some—in the Old Testament: "Circumcise yourselves to Jehovah, and take away the foreskins of your heart" (Jer. 4.4). An unclean heart cannot see God. Is your heart clean and undefiled? How many have pride, jealousy and uncleanness in the heart! If these unclean things are not taken away from your hearts, you cannot see God. All whose heart is impure or unholy cannot see God. Your outward conduct may be good, but you love the world inwardly. You commit the same sins in your heart as do those who are immoral. Do you covet others' houses, cattle, servants or wives? Unless these things are cut away from your heart, you have no portion in God's covenant.

"Behold, the days come, saith Jehovah, that I will punish all them that are circumcised in their uncircumcision: . . . for all the nations are uncircumcised, and all the house of Israel are uncircumcised in heart" (Jer. 9.25,26). The nations of old were uncircumcised in the body; the Israelites, though physically circumcised, were not circumcised in heart. So they too were to be cut off. Today, we are not concerned with physical circumcision, we only ask about our heart. Our heart is most difficult to overcome. Although our heart is so wicked, we may still deceive people with our outward appearance. Nevertheless, all whose heart remains uncircumcised cannot draw near to God. The question today is therefore not one of outward appearance but of inward condition.

"Circumcise therefore the foreskin of your heart, and be no more stiff-necked" (Deut. 10.16). What is obviously meant in this passage is for us to get rid of the uncleanness within. "Jehovah thy God will circumcise thy heart" (Deut. 30.6). Once again, the meaning here is the same as that of the above passage; namely, to eliminate uncleanness from the heart.

All these passages quoted so far from the Old Testament have dealt with the circumcision of the heart. The New Testament pays even greater attention to this matter. Romans 2.28,29 is a distinct example: "Circumcision is that of the heart, in the spirit not in the letter." What God spoke of to Abraham was but *physical* circumcision, but now He has taken a step further in asking all to be circumcised *in heart*. Whoever is not circumcised in heart has no part in the Abrahamic covenant. In Paul's letter to the Galatians, he shows us how we Christians take part in Abraham's covenant. Since God promised Abraham before the law was given, what we obtain is that which was before the law. Yet we shall be cut off and have no part in Abraham's covenant if the lust, pride and jealousy of our heart are not cast away.

Now if we were only to discuss the meaning of circumcision up to this point and no farther, we would be guilty of preaching the law instead of the gospel of Jesus Christ. We do praise and thank God, however, that we do indeed have the gospel to preach, for there

has been a way provided for getting rid of the lusts and
passions of our heart. And we would turn our attention to that provision now.

Five—In Christ Christians Have Received the
Circumcision Not Made with Hands

"In *whom* [Christ] ye *were* also circumcised with
a circumcision not made with hands, in the putting off
of the body of the flesh, in the circumcision of Christ"
(Col. 2.11). Hallelujah! Let us praise God, because this
verse tells us that we were *already* circumcised in Christ.
God's word does not say "will"; it says "were." We may
underline this word "were" many times! For in Christ
we have already received the circumcision not made with
hands. How can we explain this? Simply put, this has
been done by God. Who of us knows how unclean our
heart is? But on the day when Christ died, all these
uncleannesses were crucified and put away. This is not
something that was done by human hands nor even by
our own hands. It is Christ himself who has delivered
us from the lusts and passions of our flesh. And this
is the gospel!

With regard to our former state we were unclean.
If we say we do not see anything wrong in ourselves,
we are self-deceiving: "If we say we have no sin, we
deceive ourselves, and the truth is not in us" (1 John
1.8). A self-deceiving person is the greatest deceiver in
the world. A great deceiver deceives other people, but
the greatest deceiver deceives himself. Indeed, we are
full of sins and uncleannesses. We surmise that through
determination, resolute vows, more prayer and more

reading of the Bible, we may get better, but these will not help us to overcome. Victory does not and cannot come through determination, prayer vows, or Scripture reading; victory can only come on the day when we realize that Christ died for us and that there God crucified all our uncleannesses. This is the gospel! Today the question is whether or not we believe it. We may not feel changed nor sense peace, yet we may *believe*.

You need to see that all is in Christ, not in you. What is in you is still the old creation, but in Christ is the victory. You are joined to Him. He is the vine, you are the branch. He is the Head, you are the member of His body. By God we are now in Christ Jesus. On the cross Christ has not only atoned for our sins and given us eternal life; He has crucified this no good self as well. In Him everything has been done. This is the gospel!

It is not that God does something for you today. No, He yesterday had already done everything in Christ. If hereafter you do not look at yourself but look only to the Lord, you will be able to say, "God, I thank and praise You!" This is the gospel! Do not mistakenly think that you must crucify yourself. Nowhere in the New Testament are you commanded to crucify yourself. All that the Bible says is simply this: that you *were* crucified, that you *have already been* circumcised, that everything *is* done. The question now is, do you believe it? Can you declare that on the day Christ was crucified, you were circumcised? If you believe, this fact becomes your experience.

Suppose you look at your own self. Perhaps you will wonder why you are still the same after you have heard you were circumcised. I want you to know that Satan will tempt you by insinuating that you are just the same as before, that nothing has changed, even perhaps that what God says is not true. With the result that your faith will waver.

Are there not many who expect some God-given proof in their hearts assuring them that they are now better and cannot be touched by sins? Let me be frank to say that apart from the word of God, there is no trustworthy evidence. If you believe in God's word, that is the proof. The greatest evidence lies in the fact that God has spoken. It it not because you inwardly feel good or outwardly have changed. It is only because the word of God says that you *were* circumcised with the circumcision not made with hands in Christ. That alone will prove to be sufficient if you will only believe.

What a blunder is committed when people will not believe in God's word because they do not see or feel themselves changed for the better. This is *not* faith. No matter what your experience is, it cannot make God's word either unreal or more real. If you think you are truly circumcised but only because you have more patience today or have overcome temptation once, may I remind you that that is not faith. That is merely looking at your symptom, at your experience. You will be defeated with such a mentality. I myself have had the experience that whether I feel good or bad, I cannot be moved if I believe in God's word. On the contrary, my feet stand on solid rock, and I am as secure as the formidable mountain. If you deem yourself getting better and half-believe in yourself, you will soon fall. But by truly trusting in God's word, you will find the infinite power of God manifested in your life, enabling you to overcome the temptations and sins which you could not overcome before. You come to know that it is not you, but God, who does all this. All uncleannesses will fall away as though a piece of foreskin had just been cut off from an uncircumcised body.

God has already accomplished all things in Christ. Whether you feel it or not should not create any problem. The important thing is that you believe what God has said about you: you were circumcised in Christ, and hence you have been circumcised! You do not even need to struggle to hold on because God cares for the faithfulness of His word far more than you even care for victory. Just believe, and God will take care of its success.

How many young believers attempt to hold on to victory with their own strength, but as soon as they are tempted they fall. Then Satan will suggest to them that they are no better than before. And once that suggestion is accepted, they lose all hope. If there be a hero of faith who, from the outset of believing and as he goes through all the tests of experience, stands firm in the word that "whatever God has said, it is done," he will greatly glorify the Lord. If one can believe in God's word under the most hostile of circumstances, he brings much glory to God. Though there may be a cloud before his eyes, he ought to keep in mind that above the cloud the sun still shines. However dark may be the situation, God's word remains true. Not to believe in God's word is one of the greatest sins in the whole world.

Today a glad tiding is being given to you—which

is, that you may overcome. You do not overcome because you do not believe. If you are still troubled by lusts and passions, this can only be attributable to your unbelief and not to any unfinished work of Christ. A sinner remains unsaved not because Christ cannot save him or because Christ has not shed His blood to redeem him, but because he will not believe. If a person really believes in God's word, glorious days will come to that one. He will walk on earth conscious of the sun and not of the cloud.

May God give us faith. May we believe in His word today. And as soon as we believe, we shall instantly possess it.

4 | God's Will and Man's Willingness

> If ye abide in me, and my words abide in you, ask whatsoever ye will, and it shall be done unto you. (John 15.7)

God's children ought to know and need to know God's will. It is not right for us not to know the will of God. "He that followeth me," said Jesus, "shall not walk in the darkness" (John 8.12). This indicates that whoever follows the Lord will have the light to see and to know. Conversely, should anyone fail to have the light to see and to know, it is evident that he has not followed the Lord. Let us therefore be very careful before God about this. For whenever we do not see, we may be having a problem in our following the Lord.

Yet the difficulty with some people may not be an unwillingness to do the will of God but a not knowing what God's will is. Knowing God's will thus becomes a big problem among many of God's children. All who

pursue the Lord diligently are anxious to please Him
by doing His will. In all their actions, they will inquire
whether this or that is God's will. Such a desire and
attitude are certainly commendable. But this creates a
dilemma for them. On the one hand, they wish to do
God's will; on the other hand, they do not know what
His will is. Because of this perplexity they feel uncer-
tain in all their ways as though the will of God is
something far distant from them leaving them not
knowing what to do or what not to do. In recognition
of this, it might be helpful to briefly treat this matter
of how to know the will of God.

It is true that God's will is objective, something coming from the throne above. We must therefore seek for
it before we can know it. Sometimes it requires much
prayer, fasting, and waiting upon God. For us to know
God's will, we must lay down our own idea and deny
the activity of the flesh. Although all these are essential, they are not what we wish to deal with here. Instead, we want to touch upon another aspect; namely,
that God's will is frequently manifested in man's willingness. We want to see how man's willingness fits in
with God's will.

Actively Will

"Ask whatsoever ye will, and it shall be done unto
you" (John 15.7). The word "will" in the original Greek
carries within it the thought of "the will actively wills."
So that this verse means for us to ask whatever our will
wills actively and it shall be done to us. Some may
wonder, what if that which we ask for is not the will

of God? It would appear from this that we are more careful in speaking than is the Lord Jesus. We probably would have couched Jesus' statement in these words: "If it is according to God's will, then ask whatsoever you actively will, and it shall be done unto you." In other words, the Lord believes that the will of some believers agrees with God's will.

Paul in 1 Corinthians seems to be conveying the same impression: "If one of them that believe not biddeth you to a feast, and ye are disposed to go; whatsoever is set before you, eat, asking no question for conscience' sake" (10.27). Is it not strange that here the apostle mentions only man's willingness and not God's will?

The two passages quoted above are not meant to imply that people may act willfully or that they may do whatever they like. Not so, for these words are not addressed to people at large but are directed to the regenerated who have the mind of Christ and have received the dealing of the cross — that is to say, to Christians who abide in the Lord and the Lord's word abides in them.

Having the Mind of Christ

"Who hath known the mind of the Lord, that he should instruct him? But we have the mind of Christ" (1 Cor. 2.16). We know the will of God is objective, but the mind of Christ is subjective; the will of God is upon the throne, but the mind of Christ is within us. God's will is outside of us, but Christ's mind is inside us, constantly giving us the understanding of God's will. As

soon as a person is born again, the life of God is most
assuredly planted in him, and he also has the mind of
Christ. Whenever we receive life, at the same moment
we receive the mind of Christ. Hence we have within
us a new thought, a new mind, and a new will.

Abide in the Lord, and His Words Abide in Us

"If ye abide in me, and my words abide in you, ask
whatsoever ye will, and it shall be done unto you." This
tells us that if we abide in the Lord and His words abide
in us, we may ask what we will—that is, we may actively will with our will—and it shall be done to us.
The vital point is, "ye abide in me, and my words abide
in you." Concerning such people as this, their will is
dependable and shall accordingly not cause any problem to God's will.

A person who not only has life but also abides in
the Lord and has the Lord's will abiding in him will
know what God desires and does not desire. In other
words, whoever is regenerated and maintains uninter-
rupted communion with God will desire only what God
desires. Do we not immediately see the cross here? Here
is a class of people who have been dealt with by the
cross, thus enabling them to abide in the Lord and to
have the Lord's words abide in them. The words of the
Lord are living in their lives. And it is to these people
that the Lord says: "ask whatsoever ye will, and it shall
be done unto you." In this case, the focal point lies not
in the will of God but in what kind of people we are.

It can be said that some Christians have arrived at
a place where they are trusted by God. Because they

abide in the Lord and the words of the Lord abide in them, the Lord can trust their will; for whatever comes from that will shall be the will of God. So that without any hesitation He can say, "Ask whatsoever ye will, and it shall be done unto you."

The Experience of the Saints

Some may object to the simplicity of thus knowing God's will. Yet we do not say here that we can know God's will without seeking; but we do say that the will of God is within us, even in the life of God in us. Of course, such a word cannot be spoken to everybody, but can only be spoken to the regenerated who have the Lord's mind, who know how to abide in Christ and to have the words of Christ abide in them. For these people, their will is God's will: whatever they desire is God's desire. For whenever they desire what God does *not* desire, immediately they feel deflated within: they find no response inside, and they cannot even pray. If their own desire fails them, would God desire the same? If one day we are completely delivered from our own private cravings, then our thought will line up with God's thought and our desire will agree with God's desire.

"Whatsoever is not of faith is sin" (Rom. 14.23). This is a principle of Christian living. Let us notice, however, that the faith here is different from the faith mentioned in other Scripture passages. In other places of the Bible, faith points to a believing in God; here faith points to a believing in oneself. So that the meaning of "whatsoever is not of faith is sin" is this: that if you condemn

yourself as being sinful, how could God—whose heart
is greater than yours—justify you? If your own heart
condemns you, then you must have sinned. Yet if what
you do is right, God will give you faith to believe that
you are right. But if what you do is not right, you will
not have such faith. Although you have done it, you
dare not mention it because you sense an emptiness inside you. And thus you are assured that you are wrong.
Since your heart has already condemned you, God's
heart is greater than yours; so it goes without saying
that He too will condemn you.

When Paul suggested that if you are invited to a
feast you should go if you are disposed to go, he was
not speaking to careless Christians. Such a word is obviously not applicable to those who have never been
regenerated, nor is it applicable to the regenerated who
never have the will to do God's will and to live for Him.
It is only applicable to those who abide in the Lord and
have the Lord's word abiding in them. If you are not
to go to the feast, you will find it hard to stir up the
desire within you to go. Even if you should force
yourself to go, there will still be something in you that
weakens you; for that something in you will tell you
not to go and will give you some other advice instead.
The fact of the matter is that you are being governed
by the law of life, and therefore your thought represents
God's thought and your desire represents God's desire.
In many things, we want to do our own will and we
even have the opportunities to do so; nevertheless, as
we begin to act according to our will, immediately something within us rejects the idea. The moment we do our
will, we sense discomfort. The more we proceed along

that course the more depressed we become and the less strength we have. So that finally, we have to give up doing. This is because there is something in us which is stronger than our own will.

Frequently, God uses this inward desire to guide us. For example, you are invited to go to a certain place; and furthermore, you would *like* to go. Strangely, however, even though you want to go, you cannot stir up any excitement over the matter. You instead feel cold within. Your outward man wants to go, but your inner man is icy cold towards the idea. You just cannot go. And in case you do go, something in you will complain with each step you take. It simply will not let you go. This is how God's will is manifested through your will. Let me reiterate that such a word as this is not applicable to all people, since it can only operate in a people who have the life of God and who also abide in the Lord with the Lord's words abiding in them.

Review, if you will, the incident in Philippi where Paul cast out a demon. A maid there was possessed by "a spirit of divination" and she persisted in following after Paul and his companions for many days and in crying out, saying, "These men are servants of the Most High God." For a number of days, Paul did nothing. Did that mean Paul would not cast out the evil spirit? Should he not have cast out the spirit as soon as he had been confronted by the maid? But, no, the mouth of Paul was shut because he felt no movement within him. If he did not have any movement inside him, it was an indication that God who dwelt within him had not moved. But one day, Paul's spirit was sorely troubled. And accordingly, he turned and said to the demon, "I charge thee in the name of Jesus Christ to come out of her." And it came out that very instant (see Acts 16.16–18). Paul's troubling was God's troubling inside him. As that which was inside him moved, he spoke outwardly. And as he spoke, the demon was cast out. Because the word of God abided in Paul, what he therefore spoke was the will of God.

The experiences of many believers can bear witness to this. Sometimes it is suggested to you that you should visit a certain brother, but what is within you makes no movement. You may visit, though it is rather forced. But there comes a day when there is movement within you, and a word comes to you. You then go to see that brother, and you have a good time of fellowship with him. If we let the inside move first, we can then act accordingly outside.

When Paul was in Athens awaiting the arrival of Silas and Timothy, "his spirit was provoked within him as he beheld the city full of idols" (Acts 17.16). Perhaps some of us might say it is not good to be provoked, but the kind of provocation that Paul felt that day is actually a good thing. Upon being provoked in his spirit, Paul rose up and preached in the Areopagus. Let us note that that preaching ultimately became an important discourse which later was included in the Bible. For on that occasion in Athens, Paul bore a good testimony because his preaching came from his heart as he was moved and provoked in his spirit to speak.

On another occasion, Paul had decided beforehand to bypass Ephesus (see Acts 20.16). He could make his own decision on that matter. The Bible does not say God decided but that "Paul had determined" (v.16).

Some Christians frequently proclaim that "the will of God has led me here" or that "God's will caused me to do this or that." They appear to be more spiritual than Paul. However, we do not find Paul using spiritual terminology here, yet his determination naturally agreed with God's will because he was a person who feared God and knew the cross.

The Holy Spirit Forbids

Perhaps some will say that Paul might have been wrong in deciding according to his own will. Our reply would be that this matter is not that simple. As recorded in the book of Acts, from the time Paul began his preaching journeys from Antioch, the Bible rarely if ever explicitly states or describes the *leading* of the Holy Spirit, but it does plainly record the *forbidding* of the Holy Spirit (see Acts 16.6). Apart from the vision given him in the night (see Acts 16.9), we can hardly tell how the Holy Spirit led Paul in the positive way. What we see instead is the forbidding of the Holy Spirit in the negative way.

If we abide in the Lord, and His words abide in us, then whatever we decide is the will of God. Even so, we still have the possibility of making mistakes. But if we are mistaken, the Holy Spirit will forbid us and will not let us pass. This is something to which Paul's experience testifies.

In view of all that has been said, then, we do not need to be a passive people. In doing God's will, many Christians allow there to develop within themselves a serious problem of passivity. Actually, the will of God should never make people passive; passivity is due to men's misunderstanding of God's will. If we have truly been dealt with by the cross, and if we abide in the Lord and His words abide in us, then the will of God will be manifested within us, and we may proceed according to that will in us. And in case of error, the Holy Spirit will restrain us by causing us to be undecided and eventually lose the desire for it.

May the Lord deliver us from all misunderstanding and all kinds of foolishness, and save us from passivity. May He bring us into the place of following Him positively and actively.

5 | Blood and Worship

Having therefore, brethren, boldness to enter into the holy place by the blood of Jesus, by the way which he dedicated for us, a new and living way, through the veil, that is to say, his flesh; and having a great priest over the house of God; let us draw near with a true heart in full assurance of faith, having our hearts sprinkled from an evil conscience: and having our body washed with pure water, let us hold fast the confession of our hope that it waver not; for he is faithful that promised: and let us consider one another to provoke unto love and good works; not forsaking our own assembling together, as the custom of some is, but exhorting one another; and so much the more, as ye see the day drawing nigh. (Heb. 10.19–25 mg.)

We will discuss briefly how we should learn to worship God. As they approach God, some believers feel they are not in the right mood, some think they have not behaved well during the past week, and some realize they have not obeyed God's word or have even fallen. For these various reasons, they are not able to draw near to worship God spontaneously and with sweetness in their hearts. Hence we want to see how men may come to God in worship.

The Blood the Basis for All Worship

Many have the idea that they may come to God and worship Him because they have good works which are worthy of His praise. They cannot come and worship if they have not behaved themselves but have done things displeasing to God. Yet we need to understand that our conduct, whether good or bad, has no direct relationship to our approaching God: "Having therefore, brethren, boldness to enter into the holy place by the blood of Jesus" (Heb. 10.19). We are told in this verse that our coming to God is based on nothing else than the blood of the Lord Jesus. Neither good works nor zeal nor spiritual experience qualifies us to approach God. The blood of the Lord Jesus alone enables us to draw near to Him. If anyone fails to see the blood of the Lord Jesus as being sufficient for him to come near to God, then may I speak most frankly that he has absolutely no possibility of approaching God.

Some of us who come to worship may have sinned, some may have fallen badly, or some may have only slipped slightly. How can we worship with one accord if our coming to God depends on the spiritual condition of each person? Our hands may not all be clean; quite the contrary, we may have our hands stained or dirtied; yet we may worship God with boldness because there is the blood. Without the blood, there can be no worship. But *with* the blood, there can be. The blood of our Lord Jesus is effective not only on earth but also in heaven, not only on the cross but also before the throne. It causes us to enter into the holy place and worship God.

Some may view this as too much grace, not realizing that only through the blood may we worship. True, this is grace overabounding, but it is not too much grace. Should God carelessly forgive our sins and permit us to come and worship Him, that *would* be grace too much. Nevertheless, I wish to state that those who have better Bible knowledge, deeper spiritual experience, and a greater number of good works are not thereby more qualified than I to worship God. Every one of us who comes before God needs the blood. Each needs the cleansing of the precious blood to enable him to draw nigh to Him. God will not accept any worship of any assembly that substitutes the blood with good works or spiritual experience; nor will those who depend on their works and experience of the past week as a condition for worship know anything about worship. Let us learn to draw near and worship God by the blood.

New Covenant and Old Covenant Worship

Many maintain that the Christians of the New Covenant bear a great deal of similarity to the children of Israel. They suggest that the worship of the children of Israel was at three levels. The first level was the offering of animal sacrifices outside the tent of meeting; the second level was that of serving in the holy place;

and the third was that of ministering to God in the holiest of all. Accordingly, they suggest that the worship of the Christians today may likewise be divided into these three levels. But whoever advocates such worship as this does not know what Christianity is nor does he truly understand worship.

We know we are different from the children of Israel in worship, since all of us today may enter into the holiest of all and worship God because of the blood; but the children of Israel could not do so. The Old Testament or Covenant presents to us a picture of distance, for the congregation could not do anything by themselves. They could not worship directly. Even the slaying of cattle and sheep had to be done by the priests. They were separated from God; they could not draw near to Him. Not so, though, under the New Testament or Covenant. Each and every believer may come to worship in the holiest place. And no one may worship for other people. Strictly speaking, even our Lord Jesus does not worship for us. It is true that the Old Testament period divided the worshippers into three classes: the congregation, the priests, and the high priest. Only the high priest could enter the holiest of all once a year with the blood; none else could enter in. But today every one of us is like the high priest, because we all may enter directly into the holiest place. We say the Lord Jesus is the great high priest. He is indeed our high priest before God the Father, and we all are priests. But at the time of worship, this is not so.

Some say that Christ does everything for us since He is our mediator. Yet verses 19 and 20 of Hebrews 10 tell us that the Lord Jesus died for us so that we might draw near to God ourselves. The blood on the altar—mentioned both in the Old Testament and in the New—was, and still is for the remission of sins; but the blood shed on the cross also enables men to draw near to God. Some may even think that for the forgiveness of sin they need the blood of the cross but that for worship and drawing near to God they must depend on their works. Hence they have boldness to worship, to sing and to pray if they have done well during the week; but if they have not done so well, they consider themselves unfit to worship now. They dare not open their mouths, and they have no faith in their prayers. By so doing, though, they have devalued the worth of the blood; for we worship by the blood, just as we receive forgiveness of sin through the blood.

The Blood Mentioned in Romans and Hebrews

Romans speaks of the blood, and so does Hebrews; but what each of them says is different. Romans mentions the blood upon the mercy seat which deals with the one aspect of our sin being atoned for. Hebrews speaks of the blood before the veil which deals with the other aspect, that of drawing near to worship God. For the blood not only forgives and cleanses us of sin, it also leads us to approach God and worship Him. Some may still object and argue that they have not behaved well during the week, and therefore they dare not come to God with boldness. Then let me ask you, When will you be good enough to feel that there is nothing wrong with you so that you may come and worship with boldness? How long will you have to wait for such a day? When will your heart be able to burst forth with hallelujahs? According to your own requirements, you will not be able to worship until after you are raptured! Let us see that our worship is not determined by our works but by our trusting in the blood.

Supposing the Lord's dearest disciples—Peter, John and Paul—were to come to meet with us today, and that we would worship in the way they would worship. Let me tell you that they would come by the blood and by the blood alone. Do not think they would worship because they are closer to God and more accepted. Nothing of the sort. If any of us were to entertain such a thought, I believe Peter and John and Paul would be the first to stand up against such an idea. They would be able to draw near to the Lord only by the blood, even as we do.

Approach God with Boldness

I have heard people say they would be satisfied if they could climb to heaven and simply stand behind the door! Oh do let us realize that we do not crawl forward to worship the Lord with such fear and trembling. With boldness do we approach God. We have the authority to be His children. This is promised to us by the Lord.

When I was young, my heart jumped whenever I went to see somebody. I was afraid I would be refused an interview. I dared not knock at the door loudly lest I incurred displeasure. I did not have the courage to see people. But this is not the way we come to see God. We come with authority because we are commanded to come, just as I would boldly knock at my own door and enter in quite naturally. Let us have such an attitude when we come to the holiest of all to meet God. If we truly know the value of Jesus' blood, we will certainly come with boldness. Knowing the value of the blood is the one condition for worship. In order to have a powerful worship meeting, we need to stay beneath the blood. Even the weakest, poorest believer has the same authority to worship as the early apostles had. The value and efficacy of the blood can never be lowered by a person's work. Each time we worship, it is by the blood of Jesus. Our good works do not add anything to the value of the blood.

As we break the bread (the body of Christ), it signifies that the veil (the body of Christ) has been rent. All obstacles to the holiest of all have been removed. As we drink the cup, it signifies the death of the Lord on our behalf. His blood leads us to approach God. May I reiterate strongly that our weakness has nothing to do with our approaching God. The blood alone is the ground. If we look at the blood, we may come day by day without losing courage.

Recall how we came for the first time before God with all our sins and called upon the name of the Lord. In just such manner we may boldly come and worship God today without fear of being hindered by our works, if we only look at the blood of the Lord. May we understand this more and more. Then shall we be able to worship and praise God with one accord. By the blood of the Lord we have the authority to serve and worship our God.

6 | The Seed of God

He spake to them many things in parables, saying, Behold, the sower went forth to sow . . . When any one heareth the word of the kingdom, and understandeth it not, then cometh the evil one, and snatcheth away that which hath been sown in his heart. . . . Another parable set he before them, saying, The kingdom of heaven is likened unto a man that sowed good seed in his field . . . And he answered and said, He that soweth the good seed is the Son of man. (Matt. 13.3,19,24,37)

Verily, verily, I say unto you, except a grain of wheat fall into the earth and die, it abideth by itself alone; but if it die, it beareth much fruit. He that loveth his life loseth it; and he that hateth his life in this world shall keep it unto life eternal. If any man serve me, let him follow me; and where I am, there shall also my servant be: if any man serve me, him will the Father honor. (John 12.24–26)

One

The first two of the seven parables of Jesus recorded in Matthew 13 are: first, the parable of the sower; and second, the parable of the good and bad seeds. In the first one, the Lord tells the disciples that the seed which the man sows is God's word, which is the word of the kingdom. In the second parable, the Lord says that the one who sows the good seed is the Son of man, and that the good seed sown are the sons of the kingdom. In the first parable, the seed is the word of the kingdom, which is the word of God; but in the second parable, the seed are the sons of the kingdom who are people born of God. So that when the Lord who is the Son of man sows, He sows not only the word but also men. He comes to this world not only to proclaim God's word but to obtain a group of people as well. He will scatter this people abroad as seed.

In the Bible, we find on the one hand that the word which God has spoken is called the word of God; and on the other hand the Son whom God has sent is also called the Word of God: "In the beginning was the Word, and the Word was with God, and the Word was God" (John 1.1). This Word has become flesh and has dwelt for a time in our midst—being full of grace and truth (see John 1.14). We know from the Gospel of John that this points to the Lord Jesus. Hence the word of God in the Bible sometimes refers to God's *spoken* word, but sometimes it also refers to God's *living* Word—that is to say, to the Son of God. For God's Son is the Word, the living Word, the Word of life. When we hear Him, we hear the Word; when we see Him, we see the Word; and when we touch Him, we touch the Word.

Our Lord Jesus is God's seed as well as God's Word: "Except a grain of wheat fall into the earth and die, it abideth by itself alone; but if it die, it beareth much fruit" (John 12.24). This unquestionably points to the Lord Jesus. He is that seed or grain of wheat that is sown and dies and which then bears much fruit. "Having been begotten again, not of corruptible seed, but of incorruptible, through the word of God, which liveth and abideth" (1 Peter 1.23). The Lord Jesus is the Word of God; but He also is the Seed of God.

Let us praise the Lord for this. Our God sent His Son into the world and planted Him as seed. The Lord Jesus did not come only for the sake of *preaching* the word of God; He also came to *be* the Word of God. He is not only the preacher, He himself is also the Word preached. He is the Seed just as He is the Sower. For what God sows is not just some words; He sows a Person. So that the Lord Jesus is indeed a seed, a *good* seed.

Two

Suppose we are asked to go to a distant place to preach the gospel. You have the zeal and you are willing to go for the gospel's sake. You should know, however, that it is not enough simply for you to go and preach, because God wants to sow you as seed. Do you see this? God wants to sow *you*; you yourself are to be the seed sown.

No doubt, God will work in men through His own word. When we preach the word of God's gospel to men, we are sowing His word in them and we expect a harvest. Yet, we cannot be considered as doing God's work if we only see the word as God's seed and not man as well. It is wrong for us to conclude that we may sow seed as long as the word we preach is basically sound and the exposition we give is pure. How often the work of God suffers because the seed in our hand is merely some objective doctrines which have not subjectively transformed us to be sons of the kingdom. We are therefore faced with a tremendous problem: what kind of seed are we? For the seed of God is not just words; His seed is also you and me as a person. The good seed is not only the word of the kingdom but is also a person as the son of the kingdom. Such being the case, we need to ask ourselves this searching question—how many among us can truly serve as God's seed? How pitiful for me to have to report that our seed is mainly objective, scarcely subjective!

Whether or not we as persons can be God's seed is really a tremendous problem. For basically the Lord has no thought of merely sending out a company of people as evangelists or a group of persons as Bible teachers; on the contrary, His main thought is for Him to use men themselves as seed. He is anxious to plant as seed those who belong to Him. If this be so, we must reflect as to what will be the fruit that grows out of us if we are sown as seed: "for whatsoever a man soweth, that shall he also reap" (Gal. 6.7). People we have helped frequently turn out to be like us. In short, what we ultimately reap proves what kind of seed we have been.

Hence let us not sigh, saying, "Who hath believed our message?" (Is. 53.1) Nor let us murmur to the effect of how helpless we are because people's ears are so heavy that they are unwilling to hear the pure word of God. The real issue is: what are we? Good seed is not merely the *word* of the kingdom, it is also the *sons* of the kingdom. After we are sown by God, what will grow out of us? Are we aware of whether what we preach is merely a discussion of matters concerning a far-away country or does it relate to those things which have happened right here in our own lives? Do we find a passage in the Scriptures and then try to expound it, or do we quote that same passage because we have touched spiritual reality before God? We ought to know that there is a world of difference between these two approaches.

Many words are delivered up as but a mere dissertation: only the words spoken by those who intimately know God are truly seed for planting. Let us not tell people of the various things and teachings which our clever minds conceive; rather, we must sow into people's ears the word which we have seen and known before God. For in proclaiming the word of God, it is not so much a matter of our eloquence as it is the incorporation of Christ into our lives. Do we speak an objective doctrine or utter what we have subjectively experienced? Many can only deliver objective truths or doctrines which fail to become operative in people's lives. Only when the speaker is also the very word he delivers can he help people. For the word of God is not for mental appreciation; otherwise the clever would have a real advantage over the foolish. But God never differentiates between the clever and the foolish. When His word comes upon us, it will be tested, just as the paint on porcelain will be brushed off if it has not passed through fire; but if the paint has been burned into the porcelain, it cannot be removed even if washed with water.

How many doctrines can so easily be brushed off in people's lives! Only by the grace of God can these doctrines be made fast and secure as He burns them as it were into us by environment and revelation. God will work time and again until His word becomes that which has been deeply worked into our lives. Then we ourselves become that word. Through the discipline and the revelation of the Holy Spirit, a certain word is inwrought into one's life until he becomes that very word. And when later you meet that person, you will not deem him eloquent in delivering that word but will instead acknowledge him as being that word: veritably, that man has become the seed of God. Now it is precisely in this way that God spreads His word. Otherwise, the preaching of God's gospel descends into merely being the passing of a word from one mind to another mind. With the result that the church will become shallower and shallower and fall far short of spiritual life and reality.

Consequently, the issue before us is whether or not we can be God's seed. What part in our life may be considered God's seed? Suppose He today were to sow you and me as seed. What would we produce? Whatever a man sows, that he shall reap. There is no exception to this rule. How very sad if the fruit we produce constitutes nothing more than causing people to know a little more about facts, teachings and doctrines but failing to help them touch the Lord's life!

Three

God's purpose in sowing is of course for reaping. Let us therefore look for a moment at the principle of God's reaping: "Except a grain of wheat fall into the earth and die, it abideth by itself alone; but if it die, it beareth much fruit" (John 12.24). This verse unfolds how the Lord Jesus must die if He is to distribute life to us. We see, then, that the path of reaping lies in dying—it lies in the cross. God's purpose in sowing is to obtain fruit; His aim for a grain of wheat is for it to bear many more grains. He did not send a prophet or even many prophets to expound clearly His doctrines; He instead sent His own Son as a seed of wheat to fall into the earth and die that He might bear much fruit. Fruit bearing is not the result of clear exposition of the teachings and doctrines of the church, nor is it the consequence of familiarity with Scripture passages. It is the result of a falling into the earth and dying. And such is the work of the cross.

The cross is an experience, not only a doctrine. If there has really been death, then there will really be fruit. But if no death, then there will be no fruit. The degree of death determines the amount of life; the number of stripes measures the totality of life overflowing.

The word in John 12.24 refers primarily to the Lord himself. But in verse 25, He immediately explains to us that the word He speaks is also a principle that not only applies to His own self but is also applicable universally: "He that loveth his life loseth it; and he that hateth his life in this world shall keep it unto life eternal." Clearly this is spoken to all. Yet even more clear is verse 26: "If any man serve me, let him follow me; and where I am, there shall also my servant be: if any man serve me, him will the Father honor." This makes it even plainer that all who would serve Him must do precisely the same. Notice that this matter of a grain of wheat falling into the earth and dying is not related to atonement, since in the realm of atoning for sins we sinners have absolutely no participation whatsoever. It relates instead to the laying aside of the self life. And according to this principle, life comes out of death. This is exactly what Paul says: "death worketh in us, but life in you" (2 Cor. 4.12). Life out of death. And such is the way of bearing fruit. Fruit bearing lies not in preaching or in teaching but in sowing. As God has not sent His Son to the world to preach but has instead sown His Son as seed in the ground, so God will sow us as seed everywhere.

A grain of wheat needs to fall into the earth and die before it can bear fruit. But before it falls into the earth, it has a hard outer shell. This shell can protect the grain, but it can also hinder it from bearing fruit. The life within cannot be released until this outer shell is broken. But as the grain falls into the earth, its outer shell is gradually broken up and decayed through a chemical reaction with the water and the earth. And thus its inner life is released. The Lord himself was this very grain of wheat of which He spoke that fell into the earth, that died, and that then bore much fruit. Life out of death was a fact in the earthly life of our Lord, and so it is to be with us in our lives. Fruit bearing through death was our Lord's experience, and so must it be our experience too.

The principle of fruit bearing, therefore, is not one of simply preaching but of dying. People can know and will recognize who has fallen into the earth and died, and who has not. Whether one has died to the self life or not may be judged by the absence or presence of the outer shell. Alas, how much natural softness as well as natural hardness we still have about us. Whether it be softness or hardness, it is the outer shell of the natural self life which blocks the outflow of divine life within, so that people are unable to touch that inner life. Only through the working of the cross will this outer shell be broken.

How difficult it is to touch the real person if he remains unbroken. You may talk with him for an hour, but you will still feel the great distance between you and him. This is due to his uncracked shell. But with those whom God has stricken, pressed and broken, you touch life when you touch them because the natural, soulish part of their being has been broken. How true, indeed, that only those who have fallen into the earth and died can bear fruit! Before God, those who have passed through death can alone bear fruit; those who have not passed through death can never bear any fruit, for although it is possible for them to have tens of thousands of people following them, they still do not bear any fruit before God because they have refused to die.

To sum up, then, the law of fruit bearing is death. Without death, the grain remains alone. May the Lord have mercy upon us that we may be the seed of God. May we fall into the earth and die, that God may reap much fruit from us.

7 | The Power of Pressure

We would not have you ignorant, brethren, concerning our affliction which befell us in Asia, that we were
weighed down exceedingly, beyond our power, insomuch
that we despaired even of life: yea, we ourselves have had
the sentence of death within ourselves, that we should not
trust in ourselves, but in God who raiseth the dead: who
delivered us out of so great a death, and will deliver: on
whom we have set our hope that he will also still deliver
us. (2 Cor. 1.8–10)

What does Paul want the brethren to know? That
they may know concerning the affliction which fell
upon Paul and his companions in Asia Minor. What
kind of affliction did they pass through? The affliction of pressure. To what extent was the pressure upon
them? Beyond their power, insomuch that they despaired of life. Such was their external situation. How
about their inner feeling? It agreed with the outward

situation, since they had the sentence of death within themselves. And what was the conclusion they came to? That they should not trust in themselves, but in God who raises the dead. For this God had delivered them out of so great a death in the past, that He would deliver them now, and would deliver them in the future.

What we would like to consider here is the relationship between pressure and power. As Christians we pay much attention to the matter of power. This is especially true among spiritual believers. They often ask if a certain person has power or inquire as to how much power he has. We hear such questionings wherever we go.

Let us see what the Bible teaches on the relationship between pressure and power. First of all, I would say that these two are directly proportional to each other. Wherever there is pressure there is also power. If a Christian does not know what pressure is, he has no knowledge of what power is. Only those who have experienced being weighed down under pressure know what power is. The greater the pressure the more power.

But before we speak any further about the spiritual relationship between these two things, let us first explain the relationship that exists in the physical realm, from which we may then learn the spiritual principle. Have you ever noticed how water is boiled in the open boiler? You may have visited a store which sells hot water.* Water is boiled there from morning till night and year in and year out. Steam escapes and fills the house, yet it is not being utilized because there is no pressure. But if elsewhere we observe another kind of

---

*Such stores are quite common in China.—*Translator*

boiler either within a locomotive or on a steamship, we will find that workers build up a strong fire beneath the boiler, allow the water in it to boil, but then, unlike at the hot water store, they do not let the steam escape. The boiler in this case is made of thick steel, and the steam is continually pressed within the boiler. It begins to gather strength due to the outside pressure since the steam is not able to spread itself out; with the result that it condenses into a kind of power. And when the power of the steam is at last released through a small opening, it begins to move the train or the ship.

Now the steam in the hot water store and the steam in a locomotive are the same. Why, then, is there such a difference in power? The steam generated in the hot water store is useless, but that in the locomotive is tremendously useful. It is because in the one case there is no pressure, the steam being allowed to disperse and thus becoming useless; but in the other case, the steam remains constantly under pressure, is then compressed and channeled through an opening, and is finally transformed into great power.

Here, then, is a spiritual law or principle to be derived from the physical law. Where there is no pressure there is no power; but pressure can and does produce power.

Yet for a Christian to know what power is, he needs to know first what pressure is. Pressure was always with the New Testament apostles. They were daily pressed and heavily burdened. Many things were so heaped upon them that it could rob them of any peaceful day. But God used this phenomenon to give them power. Because the apostles were weighed down exceedingly, there was no one who had such power as they; for pressure caused them to look to God.

Let me ask, how great is your pressure? You can only measure your power by your pressure. The power of steam is measured by the pressure of the boiler. In like manner, the power of a believer can never be greater than the pressure he undergoes. If anyone wants to know how great his power is before God, he ought to understand that it cannot exceed the pressure he receives from God. This is a basic spiritual law.

You as a believer may sometimes pray, "O God, give me power." Do you know what you are actually praying for? If God answers your prayer, He will most certainly put you under pressure. For He knows that the power of life is generated from the pressure of life. A life under pressure is a life with power, whereas a life without pressure is a life without power. Great pressure in life produces great power of life, but little pressure in life results in little power of life. Yet the power under discussion here is the power of life, not the power from other sources.

Let us continue our discussion in the moral and spiritual realm and see just how exact this principle of "pressure is power" truly is.

(1) The Pressure of Sin

How many of us have some clear experience of overcoming sin? Who among us know how the law of the Spirit of life in Christ Jesus sets us free from the law of sin and death? Who have explicitly dealt with sin and overcome it? Why is it that so few of us Christians are delivered from the bondage of sin? It may perhaps be due to our inability to use this principle. We do not know how to utilize the pressure of sin upon ourselves. Instead, we faint under its pressure. We fail to use this pressure by crying out to God and looking for His deliverance. How often we must be pressured by sin to such an extent—being pressed beyond our measure so that we can neither help nor save ourselves—before we realize that we have the power to come to God and receive the victory of Christ. And then we shall be delivered.

Suppose, for example, a believer frequently tells lies unintentionally. A little carelessness and a lie will rush out of his mouth. He will not be able to overcome this sin if he has no sense of the wickedness of lies and the pain of lying, nor will he deeply feel that he is under any oppression of lies and that he has no strength to strive against it. Only when he desires not to commit this sin will he realize how much he is under its pressure. Striving against it each time only increases in him the sense of its oppression. He still cannot speak honestly. He is becoming more and more miserable.

When and how can he find deliverance from this sin? Not till one day he confesses that no matter how he tries he simply cannot overcome this sin, that he is as good as dead. He is so conscious of the pressure of this sin that he can endure it no more. The pressure at the moment is great enough, and hence the power of overcoming it becomes sufficiently great. He seems by this time to have greater power by which to come to God and cry out for deliverance as well as a greater capacity to receive the work of Christ. Then and there he will say to God: "O God, I cannot live if you do not enable me to overcome my sin through the finished work of the Lord Jesus." As he lays hold of God in this manner, he overcomes. Do you see how the pressure of sin gives him power to come to God for deliverance?

Let us use another illustration. A believer is bothered by unclean thoughts in his mind. He has no way to curb these impure thoughts. He knows this is not right, but he has no resistance nor power to pray to God. As a matter of fact, he may try to resist and even try to pray, but it appears he is only trying halfheartedly. There is no power. Why? Because he has not felt the pressure of sin yet. And hence he does not have the power of deliverance. But if he should be disturbed by these thoughts, and not once or twice but a *hundred* times, and be defeated all the time in spite of his strivings, then he will suffer the pain of confessions and of defeats to such a degree that he cannot take the pressure any longer, not even for five minutes more. And it is at this moment that he receives the faith as well as the power to overcome his sin. In ordinary days, he has neither faith nor power. But when he experiences the heat of pressure, his faith seems to gather power. Ordinarily his resistance in the past was low, but now after the pressure has grown so great, his resistance becomes more powerful.

Let us therefore remember that pressure is for the sake of producing power. Let us utilize pressure in our everyday life to turn it into power so that we may make progress spiritually. Keep also in mind that a powerful believer does not have any extra measure of power beyond what we ourselves have; he simply knows how and is determined to utilize the pressure upon him.

(2) The Pressure of Need

One brother asked me why his prayer went unanswered. My reply was that it was because there was no pressure. When he then asked why pressure was necessary, I told him that for prayer to be answered there must be pressure. As a matter of fact, I often ask brethren this question: does God hear your prayer? The answer I receive is frequently this, that after praying for three or five times the matter is forgotten. Why is it forgotten? Because they do not feel the pressure upon them. Is it not strange that this is often the case?

If you have forgotten a matter for prayer, can you blame God for not remembering it? Naturally God will not answer it for you if you merely utter a few words of prayer casually. Many pray as though they are writing a composition. It would be better for them not to pray at all. The praying of many people violates the very first principle of prayer, which is neither faith nor promise, but need. No need, no prayer. It is no wonder that people do not receive answer to their prayer. For God to answer a believer's prayer, He will first give that one a need: He gives the believer some pressure in order for that one to sense a need. And then the believer will turn to God for an answer.

John Knox was powerful in prayer. Queen Mary of England once said, "I am not afraid of the army of all Scotland, I am only fearful of the prayer of John Knox."

How did John Knox pray? He said, "O God, give me
Scotland or I die!" Why did he pray in such a way?
Because the pressure within him was too great. It was
beyond his measure, so he poured it out before God.
The pressure within John Knox caused him to utter such
a prayer.

You may not understand why Moses in his day
prayed in such a manner as the following: "Yet now,
if thou wilt forgive their sin—; and if not, blot me, I
pray thee, out of thy book which thou hast written"
(Ex. 32.32). It was because Moses was conscious of a
need. He was so pressed by this need that he would
rather perish if God did not save the children of Israel.
Therefore, God heard him.

Paul's heart was the same; "I could wish that I
myself were anathema from Christ for my brethren's
sake, my kinsmen according to the flesh" (Rom. 9.3).
He would rather not be saved if the children of Israel
were not saved too. Such a word is not lip service nor
is it mere emotional outburst. It comes from a deep
feeling caused by the pressure of need. Someone may
imitate the words of another's prayer, but that one's
prayer will be ineffectual and useless because there is
no pressure. Who will pray that if God does not answer
him he will not get up? If anyone really has such a feeling and word within him, his prayer will be heard. You
too may go and pray with such a word, but the essential thing is that you must sense the pressure within you.

In Tsinan there was a very good brother in the Lord.
He had a brother in the flesh who was also his school-
mate. He was frequently ridiculed and opposed by his
brother for his faith. Last year I preached in that school

and had a chance to talk with his flesh-and-blood brother, who nevertheless remained unmoved. Now this very good brother used to witness in school and to take the lead among the brethren there. But for a time he ceased witnessing and his face grew sad. So that I was informed by the other brothers of his condition. They were afraid, in fact, that he had backslidden. I was therefore asked to help him.

Though I met with him a few times, nevertheless on each occasion he left after only a few words had been exchanged. He avoided me. I was truly puzzled. Then one brother relayed to me that he was told by this brother the reason why he had ceased to witness: as long as his own brother in the flesh was not saved he would not witness for the Lord. On the evening of the last meeting I had there, I talked with him again. I asked him pointblank why he was acting in such a way during this recent period. He answered that if God did not save his brother, he would not bear witness. I knew he was most honest and that he was really concerned for his brother. I also knew he must have had a special burden in his heart for his brother and that he was under tremendous pressure.

There could therefore be only two explanations: either it was the enemy who was deceiving him and causing him to faint and not to toil for the Lord, or else God was indeed going to save his brother. If God gave him such pressure and caused him to pray with such intensity, then his very own brother would be saved. The pressure upon him was so great that it was beyond his measure; and hence he displayed such a trait.

After I returned home, I received from a brother

in that school a letter bearing the good news that the brother of this young man was finally saved. For not long after I had left the school, this young man's brother had become very sick. And during this sickness he had accepted the Lord and his sickness was healed!

The experience of this young man shows us a principle: before God answers prayers, he often puts great pressure upon us so as to cause us to pray. Formerly we had no power in prayer, but now with such pressure we are able to pray. The greater the pressure from God, the more powerful becomes our prayer. Let us therefore learn this lesson: pressure produces power. The purpose of pressure is not to crush us, but to be utilized by us to turn it into power.

May we thus understand why some prayers are answered and others are not. Why is it that God often hears prayers for big things while He does not hear prayers over small matters? Why is it that God hears our prayers for loved ones, friends or co-workers when they are dangerously ill, but He does not immediately hear our prayers when we have a headache, a cold or have some scratches? I have said before and will say again: any prayer that does not move us cannot move God. It is a matter of power, and power is determined by pressure.

Why does God allow many difficulties, many dead ends and many unavoidable things to come our way? For no other reason than to call us to utilize such pressure and become powerful in prayer. Our failure lies in not knowing how to make use of pressure by turning it into power.

We ought to know that all pressures are with purpose. Nevertheless, we are not to wait till the pressure becomes exceedingly unbearable before we pray. We should learn to pray without pressure as well as with pressure. If there is pressure, let us utilize each pressure by converting it into power. By so doing we will come to realize that whenever pressure arises God is going to manifest the power of raising the dead. There is no power greater than resurrection power. And when we are pressed beyond hope, we will experience the power of His resurrection issuing forth from within us.

How many times in your life have your prayers been answered? You no doubt have at least had answers to your prayers a few times. Why were these few prayers answered? Was it not because you sensed pressure, yet because it was too great you poured out your heart before God? Perhaps you had never before fasted, but on that particular day you could not help but fast. You sensed you were being pressed to come before God. You no longer considered prayer all a burden; quite the contrary, prayer for you became that day a means by which to discharge a burden.

(3) The Pressure of Circumstances

Not only sin and need create pressure, circumstances also generate it. God allows believers to pass through pressure of circumstance so that they may live well before Him. Frequently adverse situations arise in believers' circumstances. Some are troubled by their home folks; others are disturbed by friends. Some may incur business losses; others may be pushed around by colleagues. Some may be opposed or misunderstood by people; others may have financial difficulties. Why do all these things come upon them? Many believers ordinarily do not realize how precious is the regenerated life they have received. Though they are born again, they nonetheless are still ignorant of the pricelessness of their regenerated life. But once they come under pressure, they begin to appreciate their regenerated life because this new life which God gave to them enables them to overcome in all circumstances. All these external pressures can prove the reality of this regenerated life and of its power. The Lord purposely places us in adverse circumstances in order to remind us that without His life we cannot stand. The power of His life is made manifest through outside pressure.

If, for example, your heart is being pierced by a certain affair which causes you to weep in secret, and you acknowledge that you are totally helpless and beyond any comfort, you will gain complete victory if at that moment you cast yourself upon God. You will be amazed at the greatness of the power which gives you victory. This external pressure causes you to spontaneously trust God, thus enabling you in turn to manifest the reality and the power of the Lord's life. Naturally, for those who have not believed in the Lord and do not possess this regenerated life, they will no doubt be crushed under the heavy pressure of such agonizing circumstances. A Christian, however, is regenerated; and so he has a life within him which is stronger than any outside pressure. When he is pressed, then does he overcome, since the pressure of circumstances simply substantiates the regenerated life within him.

I once read a pamphlet entitled, "Be a Gas Machine." It told the story of a particular person. In the American city of Pittsburgh, the entire community at that time were using gas lamps. The owner of the gas company was a Christian. One time he began to encounter many adverse circumstances. His clients frequently accused him of things having no connection with him at all. People doing business with him opposed him and refused to give him the normal courtesies due him. So he prayed to God, asking the Lord to grant him power to overcome all these difficulties. But after he had thus prayed, his situation only grew worse.

One day an employee came to tell him that all the machines in the factory had ceased functioning. No one knew why or could find out which part had broken down. Consequently, the owner himself had to go and inspect the situation. In his examination, he found out that the machinery was all intact except that a small valve in the boiler was broken. Without any pressure, then whatever steam had been produced could still not be utilized, thus signifying that none of the machines would operate. It was at that moment that he heard a still, small voice saying to him, "You should 'be a gas machine'." Later on he testified that this gas machinery had spoken to him even as the ass had spoken to Balaam in the olden days. Praise and thank God. He also attested the fact that because the valve was broken there was no pressure; and without pressure, the lamps of the entire city could give no light. Yet the presence of pressure would cause the lamps of the entire city to shine. So he should not resist pressure in his life. He ought instead to be a gas machine.

Do let us see that the power of a person's life cannot exceed the pressure he receives. There was once a brother among us. He had refused to worship ancestors at his marriage. Now his uncle had earlier found him a job in the bank, but due to his refusal to worship ancestors he was not given the position. We all felt sorry for him, but this incident obviously expressed how much power was in him. For if I am able to stand after being pushed, this indicates how much power I have within me. An outside push simply manifests the inside strength. The power manifested from within is as great as the pressure from without.

The Bible not only tells us of the *fact* of resurrection but also reveals to us the *principle* of resurrection. The Lord Jesus Christ was raised from the dead. This is a fact. But many teachings concerning resurrection— such as knowing its power—pertain to the principle of resurrection. So that resurrection is not only a fact, it is also a principle which ought to be proven in our lives. The principle of resurrection is based on the fact of resurrection. A certain Man who was alive physically was one day crucified. Naturally He died and was buried. But He was raised from the dead. The bondage of death had no power over Him, because in Him was a power greater than death. And although this power passed through death, it was nonetheless alive since it could not be touched by death. Hence the principle of resurrection is life out of death.

Suppose a brother is in the natural most patient, gentle and loving. These are but parts of his natural goodness which could not be resurrected. Now, though, God permits his friends, relatives and colleagues to press him, piercing him and hurting him to such an extent that he is unable to endure any longer but loses his temper. At that moment he realizes that all which comes from the natural cannot pass through death (which is the greatest trial) and remain alive. And if during that moment he will but lift up his heart and pray—"O God, my patience has come to its end; let Your patience be manifested in me"—then to his great surprise, he will find himself enduring under all kinds of death. Now this is resurrection, for resurrection is the life of God which undergoes death and yet exists.

Whatever is natural cannot be resurrected after passing through death. But all which belongs to God *will* live after going through death. Many do not know what belongs to self and what belongs to God; what belongs to the natural and what belongs to Christ; what is old and what is new; what is natural and what is supernatural. Consequently, God allows death to come upon them to let them know what *can* pass through death and what can *not* go through death. And so they will know resurrection.

Why does God permit pressure to come upon you? For no other reason than to reveal to you that whatever you consider yourself as able to do, to endure and to resist must all come to nought. You are pressed to such a degree that you can only say, "O God, I cannot endure any more. My strength has been exhausted. Please manifest Your power." God will let you be so pressed as to draw out His own power. And at that point, pressure not only becomes your power of prayer but it also draws out the working power of God.

This was so with the Lord Jesus Christ. "Except a grain of wheat fall into the earth and die," observed the Lord Jesus, "it abideth by itself alone; but if it die, it beareth much fruit" (John 12.24). It is my prayer that you and I may know Christ and His resurrection power more deeply day by day.

This was the aim of Paul throughout his life. "Not that I have already obtained," declared the apostle, "or am already made perfect: but I press on, . . . that I may know [experience] him, and the *power* of his resurrection [not just the *fact* of the resurrection of Christ]" (Phil. 3.12,10). He also declared this: "We are pressed on every side, yet not straightened [this refers to their outward situation]; perplexed, yet not unto despair; pursued, yet not forsaken; smitten down, yet not destroyed; always bearing about in the body the dying of Jesus, that the life also of Jesus may be manifested in our body" (2 Cor. 4.8-10). This speaks of Paul's circumstances and the life within him. He had many great pressures outwardly, but he had also great power within him. His outer pressures simply manifested his inner power.

The environment of every one of us is ordered by God. Please remember that you are where you are by His ordering—be it your home or school or work. Whatever circumstances you are in, whether they be smooth or rough, God wants you to manifest the resurrection life of Christ. A Christian's growth depends on the way he deals with his environment. All the things which press us hard are for the purpose of having us trained to know the power of resurrection.

Who is the more powerful? The one who offers up more prayers will of course be the more powerful. But what does it mean for one to say that the deeper life possesses greater power? It means none other than that the person having more pressure has a greater ability to deal with it. So that the depth of a believer's life can be measured by the way he deals with his pressure. Unfortunately, the Christian frequently loves to preserve his natural power. He does not want to die just as Peter did not want the Lord to die. Yet, had the Lord not died, there would be no resurrection today. Many Christians view the good life as that life having few difficulties and little distress. Whenever they encounter anything painful they ask God to remove it. In the process they may live, but certainly this cannot be called resurrection.

Suppose in the natural you could endure the reproach of ten persons but no more; so you petition God not to allow you to be tempted above the reproach of ten. But God allows the pressure of eleven persons to fall upon you. In such circumstances, you eventually cry out to Him that you cannot endure any more for it is beyond your ability. Let me tell you that God will nonetheless allow you to be pressed beyond what your own power and natural patience and goodness can endure. With the result that you tell Him you can no longer endure and ask Him to give you the power to overcome. At that moment, you shall experience new and greater power which can endure the pressure of not ten but even twenty persons. You have come to realize and experience that the greater the pressure, the greater your power; and that whenever you are powerless it is because you have not been put under the discipline of pressure.

Why, then, if this is so, must any of us delay in looking to God until the pressure becomes too great? We should instead look to Him just as soon as we sense our inability. And immediately we shall receive the power needed. Hence, whenever we encounter new pressure, we should utilize it by converting it into power. Our power will grow with each encounter.

God never preserves the natural, He only wants the resurrected. He never changes the natural since He is the God who "giveth life to the dead, and calleth the things that are not, as though they were" (Rom. 4.17). Calling something from nothing is the creative power of God; giving life to that which is dead is His redemptive power. Abraham believed in God as the One who creates all things from nothing and gives life to the dead. Man would like to protect his own life, but God rejects that life. He would break it. And after a man is broken by God and confesses to Him that he is absolutely helpless, that man will be raised from the dead. And such is the secret of life and power.

When you encounter many pressures, you should ever remember that pressure is power, and therefore you must not avoid such pressures, but welcome them. For the greater your pressure is, the greater will be your power. You will overcome all and attain to greater strength.

(4) The Pressure of Work

Much of God's work must pass through pressure before there can be good results. (Let those who serve God pay special attention here.) Unfortunately, few workers have such experience, or seem willing to experience this. The faithful, however, not only have such experience but will have it even more. If you have never experienced this, you will hereafter. God will bring the work you are doing through death. It is not because God delights in death; rather, He brings the work into death in order to attain resurrection.

At the beginning of their works many of God's laborers find that numerous people are being saved through their endeavors, and their other works are being prospered and blessed as well. Strangely, though, such a situation does not last long. After a while, their works begin to fail. Those who were saved earlier are today not making any progress. Still later, not only the works seem to have stopped, even the workers themselves feel cold and dead. When they find themselves in such straits, they most certainly want to do something, but they cannot because they appear to have lost the power. They are truly puzzled. They may even begin to think they must have committed some grievous sin. They at this point are truly fainthearted. They do not know what to do. It would appear to them that there is no longer any hope, for God no longer seems to want to bless any aspect of their work.

But it is precisely at that very moment that light will come from God to search their heart. And then they will know whether from the beginning they had been working for God or for their own selves — whether they had been competing with people or singlemindedly serving for the glory of God. They will discover for whom they had *really* been working. For when a work is prospering and is successful, believers tend to feel that everything they have been doing has been for God. Only when a person's work is under pressure will that

one be able to discern if his work has been for God
or if he has mixed himself in with the work.

You who have had such an experience as this just
described know how painful it is. For during such time
you feel weighted down and dead; you are being pressed
to such a degree that you cannot but inquire of God,
"O God, why is this so? Why is nobody getting saved?
Why are the believers so dead?" You are also pressed
to ask God these questions: What am I to do? Where
should I go henceforth? You have come to see that your
former power is not sufficient to meet the present situation and your past experience is inadequate to supply
the current demand. Perhaps God will now show you
that when the work had been prosperous, you had
secretly entertained the thought of self-contentment,
had harbored spiritual pride, had been zealous for your
own glory, being eager to excel in the work over other
people. In short, you discover that many things had
been done not for God but for men, and that it was
therefore necessary for your work to pass through
death. You now realize how profitable it has been for
your work to have suffered such pressure.

Moses himself had to learn what circumcision meant
before he could work for God. At one point, God had
intended to kill him because he was not yet "a bride-
groom of blood," in that he himself had failed to circumcise his son born of his wife Zipporah who had
apparently opposed the bloody practice (but who now
did so when her husband's life was endangered) (see
Ex. 4.24–26). The Lord just would not permit the flesh
to be mixed up in His work to which He was now calling Moses. God will allow you to be pressed to the ex-

tent where it does not matter with you if the work dies, nobody is saved, and all the brethren are scattered. This is because the work—nay, everything—belongs to God and not to you any longer. At that moment you will say to God that as long as He is able to glorify His own name it makes no difference to you if He destroys the work and destroys everything else as well. Thus do you pass through death, which is the principle of first importance in God's dealings with His workers. And from then on, God will put the burden of work afresh on you.

How very different is this from what it was before! Formerly the work had been your own, you having done it out of self-interest. But now it is God's, and it does not matter whether or not your interests are being served. The work belongs to God. He should have everything. It is no longer you. So that in this new situation, you ask God to give you power so that you may do His work under such dark and dry circumstances. You recognize you have been under pressure for some time, hence you ask Him to revive His work. And before long there will be new changes! The prosperous situation will return and you will clearly see that it is not something done by you but solely by God himself through you. With the result that this pressure you have borne gives you new power to work. Formerly it was you who worked, but now it is God working, because He has brought His work through death to resurrection. Henceforth nothing can hinder His work.

How sad that many of God's workers refuse to put themselves in His hand. Let it be understood that if anyone is faithful and obedient he will not be spared from exceedingly great pressure and he will not have a comfortable day every day. Once someone asked a brother in the Lord how he spends his days in Shanghai —how comfortable are they, and whether he has any trials. The brother laughingly answered, "Is there anyone truly used by the Lord who has no trial and who spends all his days comfortably?"

Our power cannot exceed our pressure. The greater the pressure God measures to us, the stronger the power will grow within us. God works through the process of death. Without passing through death, one can do nothing. What I fear most is that many people will not utilize the pressure given to them. It will instead be like the steam in a hot water store which is wasted rather than utilized to run a vehicle. During the past two years I have deeply felt one thing: that pressure is the aid to power. If you ever have such an experience, you too will agree that all your power can only come from pressure, that the power you have in your contact with people is derived from pressure. One day when we shall stand before God, we will fully realize what pressure the Lord Jesus Christ had suffered in His earthly days, what pressure the apostles had endured in their time, and what pressure all who have been greatly used by God have undergone.

(5) The Pressure of the Enemy

Nowadays many believers are ignorant of Satanic pressure. Yet the enemy can do much evil in our environments as well as to our lives. Christians often do not understand why there are so many disconcerting thoughts in their minds and so many disturbances in their environments. Actually, some of these are permitted by God, while some are the pressuring works of the enemy.

There was a brother who habitually had wandering thoughts. He could not concentrate. It became so serious that he was even tempted to cut his own throat. When he shared this with me, I asked if such a thought had come from himself or had been given by God or had been injected into his mind by the enemy. Obviously it could not have come from God. Hence the cause of it was reduced to two possible sources: if it was not from himself, then it had to be from the enemy. I then inquired of the brother how he would distinguish his thoughts from the enemy's. I explained that if the idea of cutting his throat had originated in his own mind, he would have had to have thought about the matter. So I candidly asked this brother if he had ever thought about this matter himself or whether somebody else had developed it and had then injected it into his mind. In response to my question, that brother told me he had never thought about such things. So I told him that these thoughts must have been given to him by Satan. This is an important principle to consider: do you yourself think such thoughts or has somebody else thought such ideas out for you before it is later injected into your mind? Let me assert that only what you yourself think is yours; otherwise, it comes from the enemy.

We need not be courteous towards our enemy. The first person in the world to have been attentive towards the enemy was Eve, who subsequently brought sin into the world. Some Christians frequently try to argue with the enemy. When our Lord Jesus was on earth, what did He do when the enemy testified about Jesus that He was the Son of the Most High? He forbade His enemy to speak. Ordinary believers may not consider it serious to let the enemy inject one or two thoughts. Yet how very tragic the consequences can be should their thoughts, little by little, become completely controlled by the enemy! Their brains can eventually become the thought machines of Satan who will use them constantly thereafter. How sad that some Christians never know how to control their own thoughts. Only when we begin to learn to control our thoughts do we realize how difficult a task it is.

Concerning sickness, we acknowledge that many illnesses are the result of our violation of natural laws. But be assured that there are other sicknesses that come as pressures from the enemy. Let me repeat that I do not say *all* sicknesses come from Satan; I only say some are from him. The boils that Job had, for example, were given by the enemy and not due to Job's own carelessness concerning hygiene.

Regarding circumstantial events in our lives, some people would reckon these to be but natural occurrences. But we need to inquire: was the collapse of the houses which caused the death of Job's children merely a natural phenomenon; and was the sudden stealing of his cattle and the burning of his flock by fire from heaven merely accidental? We all know from God's record that these events originated with the enemy. We need to understand that in our lives there may be a great number of things which speak of the pressure of the enemy. Unfortunately, many believers are not aware of this reality and let them pass by undealt with.

Several brothers were distributing gospel tracts on a train. They met a Christian there whose face was all grief. When asked the reason for this, he replied that he was a businessman and that within the first several years he had repeatedly incurred misfortune after misfortune in his family as well as in his business. And he had by this time become so miserable and could see no way out that he had decided to commit suicide. In fact, he had taken this very train with the intent of taking his life at a certain location farther on ahead. Those brethren immediately recognized this as being the work of the enemy. So they asked him if he really thought these misfortunes had been accidental or whether they might have been arranged by someone in secret. After reflecting a while, this believer admitted that it did appear to him that someone had been arranging these things at the back—that it almost seemed as though a hand had been there, plotting, as it were, each move upon a chessboard. My friends frankly told him that this was the enemy's work and advised him to resist the devil. Whereupon they prayed with him right there on the train.

The brother immediately returned home, and after a while he wrote to these brethren, explaining how, upon returning home, he began to resist the enemy day after day, how he refused to accept whatever came from the enemy, and how his present situation was gradually improving. He thanked God for having been delivered, although admitting he had not yet fully recovered.

What I want to emphasize is man's failure to resist the enemy's pressure tactics. In the beginning, Satan may only give you one or two thoughts, but eventually he will corrupt, if he can, your whole being as well as your family and environment. You are being oppressed, but you do not resist. This is a fatal mistake. You should make use of the pressure to produce the power of your resistance. When you endure beyond your measure, you need to resist the enemy. At that instant you will find a way out. Often we have no power to resist Satan; but when we are pressed beyond measure we discover a power rising within us enabling us to resist him.

Hence, whenever we are being pressured by the enemy, let us not think that such pressure is useless; on the contrary, we should utilize this pressure, because it draws forth power. Let us ever keep in mind that if we know how to utilize pressure, it will not stand in our way. Indeed, the heavier the pressure the greater the power of resistance. May the Lord enable us to resist the enemy.

8 | A Defeated Righteous Man

Turning the cities of Sodom and Gomorrah into ashes [God] condemned them with an overthrow, having made them an example unto those that should live ungodly; and delivered righteous Lot, sore distressed by the lascivious life of the wicked (for that righteous man dwelling among them, in seeing and hearing, tormented his righteous soul from day to day with their lawless deeds). (2 Peter 2.6–8 mg.)

I would like to narrate the story of a man who was defeated, and yet he was a righteous man. For there are the righteous who are *defeated* as well as the righteous who *overcome*. If we are to be ranked among the righteous who overcome, we ought to take the story of this defeated righteous man as a solemn warning to us.

This defeated righteous man was Lot. He was a man whose righteous heart was daily vexed with the lawless deeds which he saw and heard. Being a righteous person, why, then, was he a defeated man?

Let us see who this Lot actually was, for he himself was neither a famous nor a wonderful person. He is known to us primarily because of his renowned uncle Abraham.

The Beginning of Lot

"Terah took Abram his son, and Lot the son of Haran, his son's son, and Sarai his daughter-in-law, his son Abram's wife; and they went forth with them from Ur of the Chaldees, to go into the land of Canaan; and they came unto Haran, and dwelt there" (Gen. 11.31). If we also read chapter 7 of the book of Acts, we will additionally learn that when Abram still lived in Mesopotamia before he came to Haran, God had appeared to him, calling him to leave his native land and kindred and go to the place which God would show him. So Abram departed from the land of the Chaldees in order to go to Canaan. Yet not only his father but also his nephew Lot followed him. We may therefore liken the beginning of Lot to a member of a pastor's or a believer's household. Because an uncle who was now God-fearing declared that he must leave Ur of the Chaldees—a city which was immoral and condemned by God—Lot therefore followed him in leaving Ur. Because his uncle Abram decided to go to Canaan, Lot himself followed him to Canaan.

According to Jewish tradition, the house of Terah was one of idol-making. In this connection, let us note that in the book of Joshua the following informatior is also given: "Your fathers dwelt of old time beyond the River, even Terah, the father of Abraham, and the father of Nahor: and they served other gods. And I [God] took your father Abraham from beyond the River, and led him throughout all the land of Canaan . . ." (24.2,3). Having heard this uncle say that thereafter he would be separated from the world and live a godly life, Lot followed by departing from Ur with Abram.

Among the readers of this message, there probably are some who may never have heard the call of God personally but who were brought out of the world by their relatives who did hear God's call. Lot himself was one who had not heard God's call; he merely followed his uncle Abram who had heard. Perhaps your father or brother or sister or wife believed first, and then you too believed. You are a Lot. It would be bad for you to refuse to follow a member of your family who believes; but it is good for you to follow in faith.

Lot was good in this regard because he not only followed his uncle, but he himself became a righteous man. We may therefore liken Abram to an old believer and Lot to a young one. They had the same faith since they were related in the flesh. The beginning of these two men was indeed most encouraging. Later on, however, they separated, and their spiritual paths diverged greatly. Why?

The Choice of Lot

"Lot also, who went with Abram, had flocks, and herds, and tents. And the land was not able to bear them, that they might dwell together; for their substance was great, so that they could not dwell together" (Gen. 13.5,6). It is always easy to share suffering, but it is hard to share prosperity. These two men came out of Ur together and they entered into Canaan together. How beautiful this was. God blessed them, so much so, that their substance greatly increased. With this increase of substance came also a problem. This land was not sufficient for both of them to dwell in. The pasture was only adequate for the flocks and herds of one person.

Though they themselves did not say anything to each other, their servants quarreled over the pastureland problem: "there was a strife between the herdsmen of Abram's cattle and the herdsmen of Lot's cattle" (v.7). Each side claimed the same grazing area. They could not dwell together because their substance was too great. Many there be today who—like these two—can leave Ur of the Chaldees together but they soon get into conflict upon their arrival in Canaan.

In passing let me say that there are a number of places mentioned in the Bible which represent the world: Chaldea, for instance, represents the confusion of the world; Sodom and Gomorrah represent the pleasure of sins in the world; and Egypt represents the world under the harsh dominion of Satan. All three places represent the world, yet each stands for one specific aspect of it. Lot was willing to forsake the Chaldea of confusion, but he was unwilling to lay down anything after he arrived in Canaan. How like many of us Christians. After we believe in the Lord, we are reluctant to lay aside fame and position in the spiritual realm. And for this reason, there is now strife in the Church.

"And Abram said unto Lot, Let there be no strife, I pray thee, between me and thee, and between my herdsmen and thy herdsmen; for we are brethren. Is not the whole land before thee? separate thyself I pray thee, from me: if thou wilt take the left hand, then I will go to the right; or if thou take the right hand, then I will go to the left" (vv.8, 9). One of the causes of Christian failure lies in not being able to dwell together. Whenever you find yourself unable to fellowship and to dwell with other Christians, or whenever you consider your relatives in the flesh as being more excellent than your brethren in Christ, or whenever you shy away from meeting Christians — all these are proofs that something is wrong with your spiritual life. Your failure to fellowship with other Christians is a sure sign of your defeat.

All the fault lay on Lot's side. Abram was the head of the household, whereas Lot was merely a young man. Furthermore, all the substance Lot possessed came actually through his uncle. He should not have permitted his herdsmen to quarrel with Abram's. Abram realized he could not strive; and this was reckoned as his victory. Lot ought to have conceded that he would rather let his own flocks and herds starve than for him ever to leave his uncle. There was only one family in Canaan that believed in God; how, then, could he bring himself to leave that family? Sadly, though, Lot did not think in those terms. He considered the pastureland for his cattle and sheep to be far more important than family unity. He would rather forfeit the fellowship with his uncle than forfeit his cattle and sheep; he would rather leave his spiritual life unedified than to suffer the loss of his substance; he would rather let go of his Godfearing uncle Abram than let go of a single herd of cattle or sheep. But what was even worse, we shall see that since his uncle now gave him a choice, he would rather choose the better of the two land areas and leave to his uncle the inferior one.

So "Lot lifted up his eyes, and beheld all the Plain of the Jordan, that it was well watered every where, before Jehovah destroyed Sodom and Gomorrah, like the garden of Jehovah, like the land of Egypt, as thou goest unto Zoar" (v.10). Here, money or wealth was now the first consideration. Earlier we witnessed a young man who followed his uncle courageously at the beginning. After a while, however, we see him tasting the favor of the world. It would appear that now Lot could rather easily set aside his faith in God and his fellowship with the saints — he "beheld all the plain of the Jordan, that it was well watered every where" — and did not mind if Abram's herds and flocks did not have good grazing areas. No, Lot only thought of his own now.

At this point in the story, I would not ask you how long you have believed in the Lord; I would simply want to tell you that today God places two ways before you. He places before you the world as well as the promised land of Canaan. And He is waiting to see how you will choose.

Lot beheld all the Plain of the Jordan, as far as to Zoar, that it was "like the garden of Jehovah." Yes indeed, it *was* like the Edenic garden of the Lord. For is this not what the world basically is? Sodom and Gomorrah represent the worldly pleasures of sins. How the people of the world seek all kinds of pleasures in sins!

"So Lot chose him all the Plain of the Jordan" (v.11a). Lot chose the entire Plain of Jordan because, like the world, it had its blessing, glory and pleasure. Was it not truly like the garden of Jehovah? Once I asked a brother who had sinned how he felt. He answered that it was a little bit like experiencing the pleasure of heaven. When one first believes in the Lord, he dare not do many things. But later, in sinning, he finds pleasure in sins. To Lot, Sodom and Gomorrah looked like the garden of Jehovah. Is that how the world also appears to us—even like heaven?

Yet we read in verse 10 that Sodom and Gomorrah also seemed to Lot "like the land of Egypt"! How interesting that the conscience of a child of God will be able to show him the difference: that the world is like the garden of Jehovah but is also like the land of Egypt: that there are pleasures, yet there are also afflictions. We need to recall that the children of Israel had been slaves in Egypt, who suffered terribly at the hands of their Egyptian taskmasters. They were cruelly oppressed and scourged. They were even forced to make bricks without simultaneously being given the necessary straw with which to make them. And this was why the Israelites had wanted to leave Egypt. How descriptive this is of those who love the world: they may experience some pleasures and blessings from it as though being in the garden of Jehovah; but their conscience gives them no joy. How many Christians today experience pleasure on the one hand yet uneasiness of conscience on the other when they sin!—experience the pleasure and joy of the garden on the one hand yet the cruel oppression and harshness of Egypt on the other!

Let me ask the young Christians: What have you chosen? The world and its pleasures? God never forces you to go His way; He simply waits for you to make the choice. Will you choose Canaan as Abram did or will you choose the world as did Lot with its affliction as well as pleasure. Where do you wish to spend your days?

What does the Bible say after Lot chose the whole Plain of Jordan? "And Lot journeyed east" (v.11b)— which in essence meant a moving toward Sodom, which in turn speaks of a fall because "the men of Sodom were wicked and sinners against Jehovah exceedingly" (Gen. 13.13). Having made such a choice, one will gradually move eastward. No one commits sin in a day; no one falls in a day. It is simply losing a little ground today and a little more ground tomorrow until a person sins and falls. For Lot, in choosing the Plain it became much easier to tend his flocks, what with water relatively accessible and with no mountains to climb. A person who moves towards the world may live quite well; instead of toil he may enjoy comfort and ease. But that person's tent is slowly moving eastward.

If you as a believer love the pleasure of sins in the world, your feet will eventually work their way towards the world. If you cannot guard your first step, you will not be able to guard your second step. Since your heart has already inclined itself towards the world, you are not able to keep your feet from edging towards it. With your eyes fixed on the world, you cannot help but walk towards it and into it. What you have chosen is the world, and accordingly, where you walk will also be the world.

"Abram dwelt in the land of Canaan, while Lot dwelt among the cities of the valley" (v.12a,b RSV). After letting Lot choose the fertile land, Abram continued to dwell in Canaan—the land to which he had been called and a land which God could bless and in which he could be spiritually edified. Lot, though, began to dwell among the cities of the Plain—an area which he himself had chosen. Are we like Abram, dwelling in Canaan where God has called us; or are we like Lot, residing in the places of our own choice?

The Borderline Faith of Lot

"Lot dwelled in . . . the plain, and pitched his tent toward Sodom" (v.12b,c KJV). At the beginning Lot probably thought that his being a righteous man would make it wrong for him to choose Sodom itself but that it might be all right to choose an area in the vicinity of Sodom—that is to say, an area near to Sodom, but not actually in Sodom. To dwell *in* that city, he no doubt reasoned, would not be good at all, but to be *close* to it might not be forbidden. Do we not also reason like this? We say to ourselves that without question it is not a good thing for believers to choose the world, but for us to choose a place adjacent to the world may not be bad. Such reasoning makes many of us to be *borderline* Christians, wherein those of the world say we are not one of them, and those of Canaan say that we are not like them either. It is true, that such borderline Christians are so close to the world that they cannot at all be said to be living in Canaan. Perhaps we need to ask ourselves today, where are *we* living?

Once when I was out in the country area, I asked a soldier why some regiments became turncoats so readily. His answer was, because their uniforms were gray. This color, as we know, is a combination of black and white; and thus it is neither black nor white. Unfortunately, many Christians are like this color of gray. They seem to be in the garden of Jehovah, yet they appear also to be in the land of Egypt. They cling to the world as well as cling to God.

Let me ask you—which side are you on? Are you a gray-colored Christian, being neither white nor black? When worldly people meet you, will they criticize you as being backward because you are too different from them? What would really be damaging, however, is if people were to say, We think that you, being a Christian, ought to be very different from us, and yet you are the same as we are! Such is the most detrimental comment a worldling could say about a Christian! Many believers are not willing to stand up and confess that they belong to Christ. They comfort themselves with the thought that it is not important for them to say so. They will not, on the one hand, let go the garden of Jehovah, and yet they insist, on the other hand, on cleaving to the land of Egypt. They consider themselves Chirstians because they go to church service on Sunday morning and spend five minutes daily reading the Bible. Yet in their lives they have no Christian fellowship and cannot lay aside their wealth of flocks and herds.

May we ask God to deliver us from this most precarious course.

Now if you just happen to consider yourself as not yet being in Sodom because you have not apostasized, let me remind you that, as was the case with Lot, your tent—like his was—is edging closer and closer to Sodom. For without the first step ever being taken, there cannot be the second step. But if what you choose is that which inclines you toward Sodom, then you most assuredly will end up there. If you choose the pleasures of the world, you cannot but sin. If you choose wealth, you cannot help but be defiled by it. You and I should ask God, Whither do my feet go? I do not know if your feet have already begun to move toward Sodom—to move in the direction of the world. Perhaps the track you leave behind will indicate that your feet have indeed moved in that direction. But allow me to say that if you have begun to put some distance between yourself and other Christians and to love the particular cattle and sheep in your life, your feet have no doubt gradually begun to move in that dangerous direction. Thank God, however, that there are yet many Christians whose tents are still firmly pitched in Canaan. May we all realize that we must resist the pleasures of the world as much as the sins of the world.

Did Lot know about the conditions in Sodom? He certainly had the knowledge, for these Sodomites were quite openly wicked and exceedingly sinful against God, as the Biblical record makes plain: "Now the men of Sodom were wicked and sinners against Jehovah exceedingly" (v.13). Yet despite his knowledge of the true state of affairs there, Lot nonetheless moved step by step in the direction of Sodom and, as we shall soon learn, eventually moved right *into* the city. As your feet draw away from other believers, your tent is bound to slowly but surely edge closer and closer towards the Sodoms of this world. You even find yourself no longer hating what God hates and no longer condemning what God condemns as your feet gradually move farther and farther eastward.

There is a proverb among Chinese Northerners which says: Fear not slow motion, but fear standing still. Ironically, standing still is what Satan is afraid of; slow motion, on the other hand, gives Satan his desired opportunity, for this is how temptation comes in. Violate your conscience a little bit today and a little bit more tomorrow; read the Bible a little less today and just a little bit less the next; pray a few minutes less today and a few minutes less tomorrow; witness a little less today and but a trifle less the next day. This is how you slide backward. Satan will not have you stop gathering, reading the Bible, praying or witnessing all at once. No, he will instead cause you to draw back little by little. He is most patient in pulling you back only gradually.

Lot Finally in Sodom

Now as the tent of Lot moved gradually and ultimately into Sodom, what danger was he confronted with? ". . . Four kings [made war] against the five. Now the vale of Siddim was full of slime pits; and the kings of Sodom and Gomorrah fled, and they fell there, and they that remained fled to the mountain. And they took all the goods of Sodom and Gomorrah, and all their victuals, and went their way. And they took Lot, Abram's brother's son, *who dwelt in Sodom,* and his goods, and departed" (Gen. 14.9–12). During the battle told of here between the confederacy of the five kings and that of the four kings, the former was defeated by the latter. In the process Lot and all his possessions were carried away.

Now he met up with this disaster because he had by this time been living *in* Sodom. At first Lot had just dwelt in the vicinity of the city of Sodom—still a believer in God, he was one who had not yet entered the city but lived adjacent to it. The line of demarcation was still distinct. Yet we know from the narrative that eventually he ended up dwelling in the city. Previously we had observed him dwelling *outside* the city, but now he has entered *into* the city. Previously you had still looked like a Christian, but now you have become a naturalized citizen of Sodom. Sin a little bit here and a little bit there, and you will draw closer and closer to the Sodom of this world. And after a while, you will begin to feel that the adjacent rural setting is not as good and profitable as the urban, that the plain is not as habitable as the city.

The story is told of a child whose mother gave him six pieces of candy which were to be eaten the next day. The child placed the candy before himself and wondered what he should do. He dare not eat them today, and yet he could not afford not to. So he began to lick each piece of candy with his lips. At first, there were six pieces of candy. But gradually the pieces of candy became smaller. Finally, the child ate one and left five, ate two and left three, and finally ate them all. Such is the way many Christians end up sinning. Violate the conscience once, and then twice, and they shall gradually move towards the world for its pleasures. Christians need to be reminded of one thing: sin is not something a person commits once and then stops. For once a sin is committed, it creates a craving within to sin again. Each time a person sins, it produces two effects: first, it gives him the pleasure of sin; and second, it creates in him a craving for more sin. Just as Lot gradually moved towards and then into the city of Sodom, so we too can gradually move towards and finally enter the cities of the world someday. Let us not deceive ourselves into thinking that we cannot sin enough to land ourselves in the world. If you and I are anywhere in the proximity of worldly Sodom we will eventually enter its precincts. It is best that we not sin. If we sin, we will not have the power to control ourselves not to sin again.

The Warning of God

Now God had not failed to give Lot ample warning concerning the future. The very fact that Lot had been taken captive after the defeat of the five kings was God's warning to him indeed that Sodom was not a place in which to dwell *any longer*. May I tell you frankly that it is quite possible that God may be warning you when there is sickness or a problem in your family or when a business failure happens to you. If you are a Christian and yet you are daily drawing closer to the world, God will in some way warn you to repent and to return to Him, even as He did Lot.

Unfortunately, however, like Lot in his day, many believers today are not sensitive. Although they become sick, have problems at home, and/or suffer financial disaster, they seem unaware that these may be God's disciplinary scourges calling them to repentance. And should they persist in their ways, they shall incur an even larger loss, as we shall see in the case of Lot.

There was once a brother who gradually became cold in his Christian walk. One day another brother exhorted him not to slide back spiritually any more. But his reply was this: "It does not really matter. Did not brother So-and-So, who was most zealous, also gradually grow cold? Now he is sixty, and his eldest son, after being graduated from college, has suddenly died; and this elderly man today gets revived again!" "If this is what you want to happen, God will grant you your wish," said the other brother. "Oh, no, I do not want *this*!" cried out the first brother.

It needs to be said that God will discipline you if you are His and you insist on remaining in the sinful world. You may be sick or have problems in your home or suffer a severe business setback. If so, you should quickly inquire of God as to whether these things have happened to you because you have left Him. And if so, you should return to where He is, just as soon as you can! Oftentimes when God's *love* cannot attract you back, God will *chastise* you. If His *word* fails to move you, He will use *suffering* to press you back to himself. For He will not let you go without making some effort to bring you back. Unfortunately, Lot did not heed God's warning, but *went right back to Sodom after Abram's rescue of him and his family.*

The End of Lot

"And Lot sat in the gate of Sodom" (Gen. 19.1). According to the custom of the Oriental nations in those days, civil cases were judged at the gate of the city (the courts of modern tradition did not exist). Prominent people were chosen as elders and judges. And they sat at the city gate to judge whatever civil suits might arise. And because Lot now sat at the gate of Sodom, it clearly indicates that Lot had been elevated. He was no longer a commoner but was now a judge of Sodom. He had advanced in worldly position. Even so is the way of sin: at first Lot was only in the vicinity of wickedness, then he actually lived within its limits, and now he had become its judge!

What was Lot's end? Although he himself was mercifully rescued by the angels of God, his wife while escaping died in mid-passage; his daughters, after their rescue, subsequently and willfully committed adultery with him one day when he was drunk; and his sons-in-law, refusing to be rescued, were burned to death in God's destruction of the cities of the Plain.

Second Peter declares repeatedly that Lot was a righteous man: "[God] delivered *righteous* Lot, sore distressed by the lascivious life of the wicked (for that *righteous* man dwelling among them, in seeing and hearing, tormented his *righteous* soul from day to day with their lawless deeds)" (2.8). Yet this righteous man had become a naturalized citizen in wicked, worldly

Sodom! He was to shed many tears over the Sodomites' wrongdoings, but he neglected to shed any tears for himself! He became "sore distressed" for others, yet he failed to be "tormented [in] his soul" over his own plight! When he saw the exceeding wickedness of the citizens of Sodom, he thought of helping them by allowing himself to become one of their judges, yet it was obviously a futile task for him (see 19.1-11). Are not many Christians today like Lot? They themselves have failed, and yet they still try to persuade others to follow the Lord Jesus!

Now we know that God ultimately decided to destroy Sodom, but He heard the prayer of Abraham and sent two angels to deliver Lot: the two "said unto Lot, Hast thou here any besides? son-in-law, and the sons, and thy daughters, and whomsoever thou hast in the city, bring them out of the place: for we will destroy this place, because the cry of them is waxed great before Jehovah; and Jehovah hath sent us to destroy it. And Lot went out, and spake unto his sons-in-law, who married his daughters, and said, Up, get you out of this place; for Jehovah will destroy the city. But he seemed unto his sons-in-law as one that mocked" (Gen. 19.12-14). This final sentence uncovers the tragic fact that Lot had no real testimony before his sons-in-law, since they interpreted his sound of alarm to be mere words of mocking to them. Who could believe there would soon be fire coming down from heaven?

"But he lingered . . ." (19.16a). How much these words reveal concerning Lot! It would appear as though Lot in these lingering moments might have been thinking: "Listen, my cattle; for your sake I parted from

Abraham; for you I chose the Plain of the Jordan. Listen, my sheep; you have been with me these many years; can I forsake you today?" And looking once again at his furniture, at his goods, at even his barns perhaps, he no doubt said to himself: "I thought I could live in Sodom for many days to come. I was thinking of building larger barns outside the city to store all my victuals, possessions and goods. Then I would be able to say to my soul, Soul, you have much goods laid up for many years; take your ease, eat, drink, be merry. What! I now have to leave everything behind?!? How reluctant I feel to forsake all these good things!" (cf. Luke 12.19)

Now the angels "laid hold upon his hand, and upon the hand of his wife, and upon the hand of his two daughters, Jehovah being merciful unto him: and they brought him forth, and set him without the city. And it came to pass, when they had brought them forth abroad, that he said, Escape for thy life; look not behind thee, neither stay thou in all the Plain; escape to the mountain, lest thou be consumed" (19.16b,17). These were the words given them after the angels brought them out of the city. Today you may be in the world, and though you may not have much, yet you too can so easily linger over the world in the face of impending disaster, just as Lot did!

There was once an elderly lady who had fifteen dollars. Daily she would count these fifteen dollars. We may laugh at her being so money-crazy. But at those today who have their drawers full of certificates and other financial documents and who treasure such papers, God in heaven will also laugh, even as we may laugh at that elderly lady. For us, fifteen dollars is nothing much; for God, drawers full of certificates and other worldly treasures are also nothing.

The Lord Jesus is coming soon. And the destruction of Sodom, as He himself said, serves as a type of the coming destruction of this world in the future (see below). If all your hope is built upon this world, be it big or small, one day all these things will be consumed by fire from heaven. One day God will destroy all. And when that day comes, no one can escape. Let me speak frankly here, that what today believers may be reluctant (as was Lot) to give up will have to be given up on that day. At the time of rapture, God only raptures people, not things. Hence let us be willing to let go of everything today.

"But [Lot's] wife looked back from behind him, and she became a pillar of salt" (19.26). Lot's wife persisted in her husband's desire: she looked back. Although she could no longer see her things, she still craved to look upon the place where she had lived; but now it was going up in smoke. Oh, the backward gaze of her eyes betrayed where her heart truly was. Oh, this looking back revealed many untold stories and betrayed many inward feelings! And in looking back, she became a pillar of salt. It serves as a huge and solemn warning even to this day! — for our Lord declared this: "in the day that Lot went out from Sodom it rained fire and brimstone from heaven, and destroyed them all: *after the same manner shall it be in the day that the Son of man is revealed. . . . Remember Lot's wife*" (Luke 17.29-32). At the time of the second coming of the Lord, this world will be judged, and all the things on

earth will be burned. All who love the world will likewise
stand as pillars of salt just as did Lot's wife long ago.

I believe we Christians pay too much attention to
things that are trivial and neglect the things eternal.
We are busily occupied with social functions, business
transactions, and children's education. We should indeed attend to our children's education and to our
necessary business; but we must still take care of eternal things. I especially wish to address a few words to
the young people. The road ahead of you may yet be
long. If the Lord should delay His return, then choose
the right way you should go. Pay special attention today to things that are valuable, eternal, and of God.
Do not expect any glory today, but learn to draw near
to God that you may finish the course well that lies
before you. And to all of us I would echo the solemn
words of our Lord Jesus: "Remember Lot's wife"!

9 | Gleanings from Enoch

Enoch was an Old Testament character from whose life we can glean something very helpful. We do not know exactly when he repented or what kind of life he had lived before he turned 65 years old. We know, however, from the Biblical record that he began to walk with God after he fathered Methuselah in his 65th year. From that moment onward his life underwent a drastic change ("Enoch lived sixty and five years, and begat Methuselah; and Enoch walked with God *after* he begat Methuselah"—Gen. 5.21,22). Possibly it was because he had seen a prophecy. He lived on earth a total of 365 years (see 5.22b,23), but during the last 300 of those years he "walked with God." And hence, the birth of his son must have had a deep effect upon him. Moreover, if we carefully compute the years Methuselah lived, we will discover that the Flood catastrophe began to occur exactly in the year he died. So that evidently, at the birth of his son Methuselah, Enoch had been shown by God the terrible coming tribulation that was to befall the earth. He was awakened and moved by the fear of God.

It is interesting to note that while Noah preached righteousness Enoch preached judgment. Noah preached the way of salvation because God told him to build an ark of safety. Enoch preached judgment because this was what his son bore witness to. We can only preach that which has affected us inwardly. By faith, Noah prepared the ark. By faith, Enoch reaped the benefit of walking with God.

We would do well to know that sinners will be judged, the flesh will be judged, and the world will be judged: "the day of the Lord will come as a thief; in the which the heavens shall pass away with great noise, and the elements shall be dissolved with fervent heat, and the earth and the works that are therein shall be burned up" (2 Peter 3.10). Will we love the world if we truly know that such is its end? Have we ever heard of a man who, knowing that a certain bank was going bankrupt, would purposely deposit his money in it? If he knows the impending bankruptcy of that bank, he will never deposit any money into it. In like manner, then, we who know what the end of the world shall be—even its being burned up—should never love it again. Enoch perceived the meaning of Methuselah and was therefore awakened to spiritual things, walked with God ever afterwards, and was eventually raptured to heaven, as the Genesis account of his later life tells us: "Enoch walked with God: and he was not; for God took him" (5.24).

The Environment of Enoch

Can one ever say that because Enoch's environment was better than that of others that this was the cause for his walking with God? I do not believe so, for let us look into his family situation: "Enoch walked with God after he begat Methuselah three hundred years, and begat sons and daughters" (5.22). Some people have the idea that it is natural for a preacher to walk day and night with God, but for those who are burdened as they are with many family affairs, it is impossible to do so. Yet notice what the Bible tells us about the first man who walked with God: he walked with Him, and yet fathered many sons and daughters who needed to be cared for. Others maintain that they cannot walk with God because they must work long hours in factories and be surrounded by the noise of many machines. Enoch, however, as he walked with God for three hundred years, was not without the burden of the noise of many children. The life we receive is not supposed to be manifested only in a good or pleasant environment; it is given to be manifested in any and every circumstance whatever. This is not a matter of merely walking with God under good environment; it is a matter of being able to walk with God at all times and under any condition. Many children and many family burdens cannot hinder a true believer from walking with the Lord: that no matter how heavy these family burdens and responsibilities are (and they indeed are not light!) he will not be entangled by these things as unbelievers usually are: he is able to walk with God under any such circumstances.

Let us notice, furthermore, that the time in which Enoch lived was a very dark period. In Enoch's day, Adam was still alive. And from Genesis 4 we know that the descendants of the seed of Cain were also still present on earth. What was their condition? "Lamech took unto him two wives: the name of the one was Adah, and the name of the other Zillah" (v.19). Lamech was the first man who broke God's rule of there being but one husband with one wife. Ever afterwards throughout the earth the custom of polygamy was to spread. Adah means "pleasure" or "adornment" or "the decorated." This would indicate that the women of that period were becoming fashion-conscious; they were inclining towards luxury. "And Adah bare Jabal: he was the father of such as dwell in tents and have cattle" (v.20). This is the first mention of how men would profit through cattle raising. "And his brother's name was Jubal: he was the father of all such as handle the harp and pipe" (v.21). By this time men had already begun to pay attention to music and amusement. "And Zillah, she also bare Tubalcain, the forger of every cutting instrument of brass and iron" (v.22). Such cutting instruments of brass and iron were beginning to be fashioned as weapons of war. Hence war must have had its beginning at that time too. Now in the midst of all these conditions, we read that Enoch walked with God.

Licentiousness, profit-planning, fashion and dress, amusement orientation, and weapon manufacturing—are not all these the phenomena of our own days? Yet God shows us here how Enoch in his day was able to walk with Him for 300 years in such a time as that! How about us today? Are we walking with God? G.

H. Pember of England was one who knew the Lord deeply. Several decades ago he prophesied that people in the world would henceforth pay more attention than before to music, higher knowledge and weapon manufacturing. We know that all of this is true today. It would be well if, under such circumstances as these, we could begin to walk with God today as Enoch did in his day.

The Rapture of Enoch

"By faith Enoch was translated that he should not see death; and he was not found, because God translated him: for he hath had witness borne to him that before his translation he had been well-pleasing unto God" (Heb. 11.5). How was Enoch translated or raptured? By *faith*, says the writer of Hebrews. Wherein had he been well-pleasing to God? He had walked for 300 years with Him. Before his rapture Enoch had already had witness borne to him that he had pleased the Lord. By walking with God, he had pleased God. And by faith, he was taken by Him. Each one of us must so walk till we too will receive the witness that we have been well-pleasing to God. And then by faith we too shall be raptured.

Every believer will be raptured, but the first to be raptured must be the overcoming believers. Only those who are ready and waiting for the Lord will be raptured first. If you do not believe, you will not be raptured. You must believe you will be raptured, otherwise you will not be raptured. May God give us the faith of rapture!

It is most amazing that Enoch had this faith. One reason for his faith was because he walked in good conscience with God. Faith and conscience are connected. When conscience is breached, faith is destroyed. Faith will leak out through the breach made in one's conscience; and without faith, there can be no rapture. Why do many believers not believe in rapture? Because they do not walk with God. If we walk day by day with our God, we will be given the faith of rapture. The words of Hebrews 11.6 follow immediately upon those of verse 5: "And without faith it is impossible to be well-pleasing unto him; for he that cometh to God must believe that he is, and that he is a rewarder of them that seek after him." We are told here that we must believe two things. First, we must believe that "God is"—that is to say, we must believe that God is what He says He is. Second, we must believe that God will reward all who seek after Him. By this verse, then, we know that Enoch's faith had these two elements: first, he believed that God was what He said He was; and at the same time he sought diligently to walk with God, believing that he would be rewarded. Enoch sought to be delivered from the future tribulation that was intimated to him at the birth of his son, and so God rewarded him with rapture.

Have we ever asked God to deliver us from the great tribulation which is coming upon the whole earth? Note what Jesus urged his disciples to do: "Watch ye at every season, making supplication, that ye may prevail to escape all these things that shall come to pass, and to stand before the Son of man" (Luke 21.36). Many take this word of our Lord to mean that those who watch and pray God will deliver from the coming great tribulation. But this is actually a call to specific prayer; namely, that believers should watch and pray at every season for God to deliver them from the great tribulation to come. Now this was truly Enoch's prayer. And whoever else today prays such a prayer will also be raptured. In waiting for the return of our Lord, let us earnestly ask God to deliver us from the coming great tribulation. With each passing day the rapture is getting closer. Let us walk before God with a conscience void of offense, waiting singlemindedly for the rapture. So shall we believe in God, and so shall we pray to God. Today is the time in which He prepares us.

Do we believe we shall be raptured? Do we pray that we may be delivered from the great tribulation to come? How many of our prayers have been answered? We should at least have this prayer answered! Let us keep praying at all times until God answers us *this* prayer.

Concerning this matter of walking with God, it is good that we start well and continue well, but it is highly important that we end well too. Many begin well in walking with God, but unfortunately their ending is not in glory. Many are frightened when they hear about the great tribulation and judgment to come. Yet it needs to be seen that rapture is not something which suddenly happens in history. The fact of the matter is that rapture occurs only after a walking day by day with God until you are taken by Him, just as the Genesis record says of Enoch: "Enoch walked with God: and he was not; for God took him" (5.24). The change which is to come "in a moment, in the twinkling of an eye"—as spoken of in 1 Corinthians 15.52—has reference to the body, not to life. To be raptured is a matter of walking together with God and not that of taking flight. Let us walk and walk and keep walking with the Lord right into glory!

One brother has observed that the experience of a Christian is chain-like—it is the chain-links of death, resurrection and rapture, repeated over and over again; chain after chain until the Christian reaches glory: one more death means one more filling of resurrection life, which in turn means a coming nearer and nearer to rapture. Let me repeat, that rapture is not merely a historical point-action event in time: it is additionally an experience that builds up gradually until it automatically and instantly culminates in glory.

Enoch walked with God for 300 years. And by the time he was raptured, he was unquestionably quite familiar with God. One brother has said that unfortunately many when they arrive in heaven will feel strange in God's presence because by that time they shall not have conversed much with Him on earth! Oh, day by day let us walk step by step with God until we are wholly sanctified. May God be gracious to us that we may walk daily with Him as Enoch did. For if Enoch could do it, is there any reason why we can not do so too?